DESIGN BASICS
FOR RUG HOOKERS

SUSAN L. FELLER

Copyright© 2011 by Stackpole Books

Published by
STACKPOLE BOOKS
5067 Ritter Road
Mechanicsburg, PA 17055
www.stackpolebooks.com

Customer Service (877) 462-2604
www.rughookingmagazine.com

All rights reserved, including the right to reproduce this book or portions thereof in any form or by any means, electronic or mechanical, including photocopying, recording, or by any information storage and retrieval system, without permission in writing from the publisher. All inquiries should be addressed to *Rug Hooking* magazine, 5067 Ritter Road, Mechanicsburg, Pennsylvania 17055.

Cover photographs by Impact Xpozures.
On covers: *Three Elements of Design*, designed and hooked by Mary Jane Peabody.
Photographs by Susan L. Feller unless otherwise noted.

Library of Congress Cataloging-in-Publication Data

Feller, Susan L.
Design basics for rug hookers / Susan L. Feller.—1st ed. p. cm.
"Rug hooking."
   ISBN 978-1-881982-77-7
    1. Rugs, Hooked—Patterns. I. Title.
   TT850.F45 2011
    746.7'4—dc23
2011024852

CONTENTS

Dedication v
Acknowledgments vi

SECTION ONE:
Introduction
Chapter 1
Creativity 1

SECTION TWO:
Building A Foundation—The Elements
Chapter 2
Texture and Value 5
     Exercise #1: Creating Texture
     Exercise #2: Arranging Value

Chapter 3
Line and Shape 10
     Exercise #3: Drawing Lines
     Exercise #4: Using Shapes

Chapter 4
Form, Space, and Scale 14
     Exercise #5: Adding Dimension
     Exercise #6: Showing Depth

Chapter 5
Color 19
     Exercise #7: Reacting to Color

SECTION THREE:
Make Your Own Art—The Principles
Chapter 6
Pattern, Contrast, and Emphasis 26
    Exercise #8: Repeating Patterns
    Exercise #9: Emphasizing Contrast

Chapter 7
Rhythm and Movement 33

Chapter 8
Balance and Unity 36
    Exercise #10: Balancing Motifs

SECTION FOUR:
The Gallery
Chapter 9
Gallery of Rugs 39

SECTION FIVE:
Skill Building
Chapter 10
Composition 69

Chapter 11
Transferring a Design 73
Mountain Treeline Pattern

Chapter 12
Borders, Finishing, Framing Tips 76

Illustrated Glossary 85
Resources 89

DEDICATION

To the women in my life who worked with their hands and shared those skills:

Grandma Louise Young, Aunt Jo Barnes, and my mother, Carol Feller.

You gave me roots, independence, and a drive to inspire.

ACKNOWLEDGMENTS

Along a journey you meet people who influence and affect the rest of the trip. Stephanie Allen-Krauss and Linda Rae Coughlin are friends and textile artists, and, in their own ways, have mentored me. Thank you for encouraging me to develop teaching skills, networking, and promotion within the world of rug hooking.

The students during 2009 and 2010 at Green Mountain Rug Hooking School, East Randolph, Vermont; Loyalist College in Belleville, Ontario; and Bev Stewart's *Whispering Pines*, Clayton, Indiana, all jumped in to explore and learn. Your input and artistic approaches to the basics encouraged me. Especially thank you to Francine Even and Christine Walker-Bird for wanting to learn more, you and I have.

Debra Smith, you opened the door and I stepped through. Thank you for coming along with editorial guidance and friendship on this journey.

To the talented artists whose works are included here, may your contributions of designs, materials, and techniques inspire creativity.

And heartfelt thanks to Jim Lilly for keeping the home fires burning.

CHAPTER ONE

Creativity

"To see is itself a creative process, requiring an effort."
—Henri Matisse (1869–1954)

Believe in Yourself, #4- and 6-cut wool on linen. Designed and hooked by Ellen Banker, Barnard, Vermont, 2010.
NEIL STEINBERG

Can't draw a straight line? No problem. Learn how to create. If you picked up this book and thought, "I can't even draw a straight line, how can I design," don't worry. My goal is to teach you the basics of design. If you have created your own designs or changed a commercial pattern, or if you have chosen your own colors for a rug, you already know the thrills and pitfalls of the design process. This book can help you become more confident in using the right techniques, selecting materials, and arranging elements for a dynamic composition. In any case, what you need to bring to the table is a desire to learn. So let's set some reachable goals and begin to learn.

SUPPLIES

Gather supplies, such as pencils, a camera, and a journal.

- Journal with blank paper to gather notes, sketches
- Collection of art books, photos, magazine and catalog cutouts
- Color wheel
- Digital camera
- Sheet of red acetate, or some other way to view wools as value not color
- Colored pencils: red, yellow, blue, orange, green, violet, black, and several values (shades) of gray
- Pencil, preferably #2 soft, and eraser
- Drawing tools, such as a ruler or compass
- Black markers, ultra-fine and fine points
- White paper, 8 1/2" x 11"
- Colored paper: several sheets of red, yellow, blue, orange, green, violet. Look for bundles of paper that include a variety of values.
- Scissors
- Glue stick or tape
- Pro-Chem dyes 119, 338, 440 and 135, 351, 490, and 672; or a full set of Majic Carpet Dyes; or a selection of colored wools in solids, textures, and light-to-dark values
- Wools: natural, white, textured in a variety of light to dark patterns
- Rug hooking tools: frame, hook, scissors, cutter

Books are a great source of knowledge and inspiration.

To create the exercise samples, you'll need a variety of drawing paper and a color wheel.

You'll also need a selection of neutral wools.

2 ■ DESIGN BASICS FOR RUG HOOKERS

MAKING THE SAMPLES

Throughout this book, you'll be designing several mats to emphasize certain aspects of the design process. I suggest the following kits for each:

- 1 woolen 8-value swatch of one color
- 6 pieces of neutrals, from light to dark, including solids and textures
- 3 pieces of another color (If the swatch is a primary, select its complement.) Include solids and textures to increase value range
- Scrap bag of cut strips (a variety of widths, yarns, fibers)
- Backing material of choice (Begin with a 20" x 20" piece which will make four 5" squares, measuring at least 3" from the backing edge and giving 4" in between squares.)

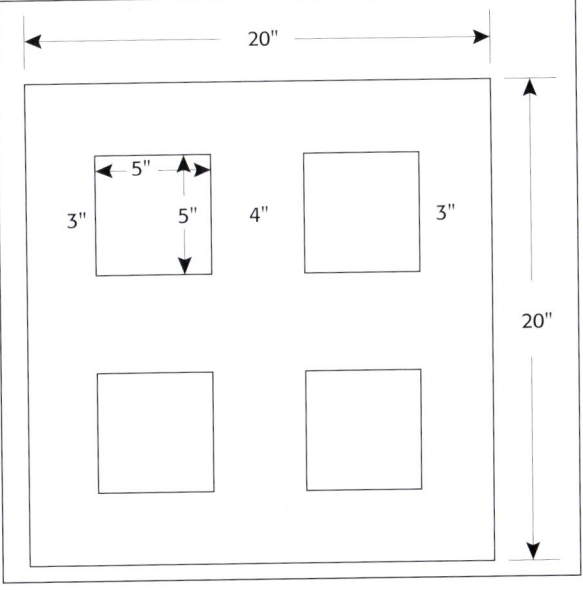

A stool can stand on three legs. Let's think of a successful piece of work as a stool needing these three legs: technique, materials, and design. Learning rug hooking techniques takes time, dedication, and a willingness to improve your skills and develop your own personal style. Workshops, books, experiments, guild meetings, and exhibits inspire us to learn new ways to manipulate fabric. Throughout the book, you will use your repertoire of rug hooking **techniques** to emphasize the design.

Materials for rugs need to be sturdy. Washed or fulled wool is most commonly used for hooked rugs because the interlocked fibers stand up to stress and abuse, and therefore wear evenly. While we cut apart the structural weave of wool yardage, the unique characteristics of wool's scales to knit around each other strengthens the fibers. The texture, color, and width of the wool strips all affect your design. (See chapter 2 to learn about texture and value.)

Likewise, the materials for the backing of a rug need to be just as sturdy. Without a strong backing, even the best wool will not keep its shape in a rug. Monk's cloth and linen are two types of fabric that are most often used as foundations.

A **design** refers to the full composition (rug pattern) and to the style used in arranging parts. The parts are our elements of design: line, shape, form, space, value, texture, and color. The ways the elements are arranged are considered the principles: pattern, contrast, emphasis, rhythm, movement, balance, and unity. It is the orderliness of the elements and principles that results in a superior design and the well-deserved comment, "What a great rug!"

For your next project, ask yourself what message you want to convey.

- Is it emotional? Learn what colors and placement of objects will communicate the feeling. For example, see *Peace on Earth* in chapter 9 (page 62). All parts of this rug—from the colors to the placement of the houses—work together to convey a feeling of calm.

- What is the purpose? A room-sized rug needs to work with furniture and/or a traffic pattern. A small scatter rug accents a space. The scale (size) of the motifs should draw attention from a distance and bring the viewer closer for a look.
- Learn how different materials, unusual motifs, and a bright or strongly contrasting value range all add to the shelf life (success) of a powerful design. Remember this formula:

Elements + Principles = Visual Language

After experimenting with the exercises in this book, you will be able to identify the elements and principles in your next pattern, make material choices, and use techniques to communicate through a unique work of art, your own "great rug."

USING THIS BOOK

Let's go back to the "I can't draw" comment. Do you remember learning to read, write, cook, or hook? You took lessons starting with the fundamentals. A skill is developed with small building blocks, repetition, and using your senses in different ways. Take each chapter in this book as a step, repeat and add new lessons, and gradually your craft will improve. Actively working the samples will build knowledge and confidence. You'll be on the way to becoming an artist.

To get the most out of this book, use each chapter in the following ways:

- Study the terminology
- Do the exercises
- Hook the samples
- Answer the questions to review
- Use the gallery of rugs in chapter 9 to challenge your knowledge

First of all, take a quick look through the book to get a sense as to how we will proceed. After you've skimmed through the book, gather your supplies so you're ready to work creatively and efficiently without being interrupted by a search for wool or a hook.

Throughout the book, you will see many 5" samples; some are hooked by my students, some I hooked myself to illustrate concepts and demonstrate techniques. In the interest of brevity, I've included only the name of the piece if I hooked it. Those squares hooked by others will have their names and the name of the piece in the caption.

A POSITIVE RELEASE OF CREATIVITY

There are no rules for the exercises I've included in this book, just lessons to learn from looking and seeing. You look at rugs and react positively or negatively based on your own personal past experiences. "Seeing" is when emotions are involved and you react emotionally. All of our "seeing" builds our experiences so we look at the next image differently.

Keep in mind that people have visual dialects as we have verbal dialects. To a person from the eastern United States, a carbonated beverage is soda; in the Midwest the same drink is called pop. If I say, "Draw corn," a farmer may sketch a cornstalk with cobs in a field; a city dweller may draw a single cob on a plate. This illustrates how we all see art differently and why we should not use accusing, negative words in response to another's work.

Einstein is quoted as saying, "Imagination is more important than knowledge." I include this quote to remind us to release any negative thoughts and become more childlike. In the upcoming samples, take advantage of accidents and remember to experiment. Over time, let the *process* of rug hooking overpower the *object*, and let your confidence grow.

Writing this book was a fascinating year of discovery. That year was a natural result of my five decades of experiences and studies. Piles of books, hooked samples, and collected examples surround me tonight as the book grows. I have to focus and select words and pictures to describe each step along the way. It is overwhelming and exciting . . . and I am sharing this with you to encourage you to start your own creative journey. It's time to begin.

How?

Simplify . . . and turn the page.

CHAPTER TWO

Texture and Value

"The first two things to study are form and values. For me, these are the basis of what is serious art." —Jean Baptiste-Camille Corot (1796–1875)

The first two elements are texture and value. Texture: because we use fabrics and select them by touch—tactile texture. Value: because light and dark areas attract the eye and give depth to a piece.

TEXTURE

Texture is the quality of a surface. In visual art, there are two types of texture: tactile and implied. **Tactile texture** is the way the surface of an object feels. Is it smooth or rough, fuzzy or slick? When we look at a piece of wool—or hooked rug—we invariably want to touch it. **Implied texture** is the way artists make the viewers' eyes see the surface—how a texture is *suggested*. The eyes take that suggestion to the brain and we recall how that texture feels. For example, if you hook a cat's fur in the same direction that the animal's fur grows, you will involve the viewer more personally. A folk artist could address a cat image as a flat object by using textured wool to give the effect of fur, or added lines for a raggedy edge.

What are textured wools? Mills and weavers arrange yarns of different colors and values in particular patterns to create textures. Plaids, herringbones, tweeds, houndstooth, and checks are some of these weaves. They are produced in both bold and minimal proportions, with very strong contrast in value or only subtle differences, like in Dorr's oatmeal. Rug hookers love to use these fabrics. Cynthia Norwood, Barb Carroll, Jayne Hester, and so many others focus on using textures effectively in their work.

Winter in West Virginia, detail. (See the full rug on page 58)

Dorr Mill oatmeal is a versatile, subtly textured wool.

HOW TO USE TEXTURED WOOL

Use the following tips when you're working with textured fabrics in the upcoming lessons:

- A plaid, when cut into strips, can be separated into distinct piles according to value and color.
- The looser weave of many textured wools means it is difficult to use them as fine cuts. Even if you wash the wool several times to full the fibers, the structure may fall apart. Expect to use a #5 or wider cut for textured wools. ▶

▶**TIP:** As you work through this book, keep a journal or stack of paper handy to jot down definitions and make notes to yourself.

■ EXERCISE #1 *Creating Texture*

Try translating an interesting patch of bark into a two-dimensional sketch as a study in texture.

LEARN: Take out a piece of paper or your journal and a pencil. Section the page into four parts. In each section quickly sketch a visual interpretation of the following phrases:

- moving rain
- craggy bark
- pointy grass
- pebbled sand

No one will see these but you; so don't hesitate and don't over-think—just draw. Label each drawing as to what it is.

Now think about what you did: Did you use your pencil in different ways? Did you use heavy, wider lines for the crags in the bark and thin, long, diagonal ones for driving rain? Maybe you made a series of small dots for pebbles of sand and short vertical strokes of varying widths for the grass. How did you use your tool, the pencil?

Square Tree Trunk, 5" x 5", wool on backing. Designed and hooked by Mary Anne Keast, Belleville, Ontario, 2010.

APPLY: To translate your sketches to hooking, think of the lines on your sketches as strips of wool. Choose a cutter blade width for each type of line you drew. Translate the pencil lines into hooked lines: Maybe you will select heavy, dark, textured pieces to accentuate the crags of bark; pick light, thin pieces for the rain; and medium to dark strips behind the rain drops.

HOOK: Look at your sketches again and choose one word to describe a feeling associated with each sketch. Now consider what materials you could use to emphasize that feeling. You might think of loneliness to describe the cold, driving rain. Think of dark textures against a plain background. Now draw your word as a design onto one of the small 5" squares and hook it, using only the neutral fabrics. No color allowed in this first piece.

- Wider cuts often work quite well. For example, sometimes a group of colored threads, as wide as a #2 cut, will fall exactly in the middle of a #6 cut, resulting in the look of three #2 cuts. Use this visual line to your advantage.
- When working with wider cuts and textures, your loops will be more noticeable. This aspect adds interest and dimension to the design.
- The smaller a check or houndstooth is, the closer to medium value it will hook up.
- With two pieces of wool equal in value, one textured and the other a solid, the textured one will visually recede and the solid one will advance.
- Use textured wools to emphasize depth.
- Washing wools reduces their luster: washing will lower the value (darken) and intensify (deepen) the color of the original unwashed fabric.

How can we suggest texture in hooked rug designs? Artists portray texture by arranging lines. A series of long and short lines coming out from the edge of a cat's outline helps us to "see" a furry cat. Adding a few loops of different values in a solid area will break up the flat surface, adding interest.

We have an advantage over artists who create on paper because our medium can be manipulated to exaggerate implied texture with tactile texture. We can vary the heights of our loops, cut the strips thin or wide, clip to sculpt a soft round berry, or prod a lion's mane with long pieces.

VALUE

Value refers to the relationship between light and darkness on a surface or object. Value helps create form by giving objects depth and perspective.

"If I could have had my own way, I would have confined myself to black and white." —Edgar Degas (1834–1917)

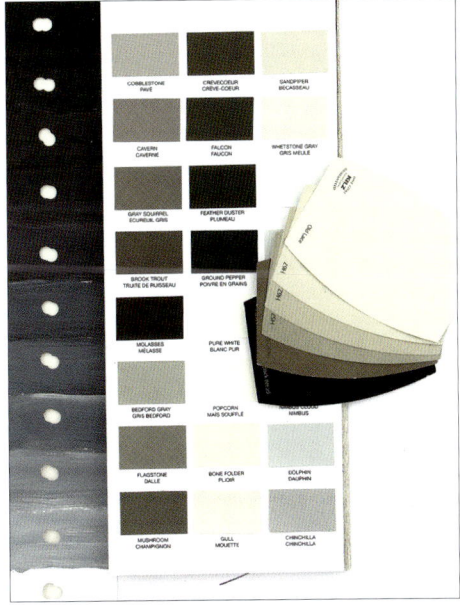

Olympic Peninsula, detail. (See the full rug on page 59.)
Left: Examples of value scale.

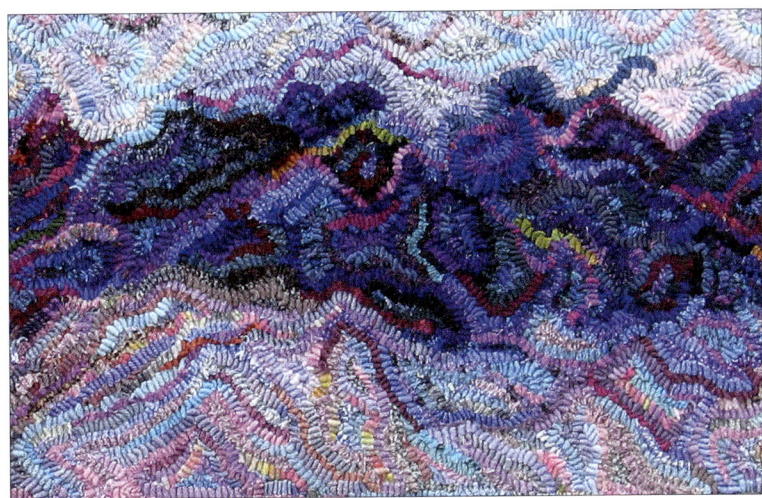

My Mountain State, detail. (See the full rug on page 54.)

Geometrics for Tamarack, detail. (See the full rug on page 54.)

Value is an incredibly important tool. With it you can portray space, shape, and movement, and attract attention to a specific object. Once you understand value, you will know that combining value with color knowledge will make art sing. I hear people say, "I want to learn more about color" or "I have problems color planning." If you understand how to use value, color will become easier.

How much physical light is in a picture and where the source of the light is will determine the value of

▶ **TIP:** When we dye to achieve changes in value, we add more of the dye formula to the same amount of fabric, darkening each batch. A value swatch is created with the lightest swatch referred to as #1, numbering each succeeding color on through to the darkest. (For easy instructions on how to make value swatches, I recommend *Primary Fusion* by Ingrid Hieronimus.)

TEXTURE AND VALUE ■ 7

DORR SWATCH SET

Values are easy to define when they're shades of brown or black—what we call neutrals. If you're having trouble grasping values when it comes to colors, try this exercise and then check your progress by converting everything into a neutral with one of these tricks.

- Take your scrap bag of colorful strips and sort out three piles: light, medium, and dark. How successful were you in sorting?

- Did you have problems determining into which pile some pieces needed to go? If so, get out your digital camera and put the setting on grayscale or on black and white. Now look through the lens—you don't even need to snap the picture, just looking through the lens on this setting will show you what you need to see. Can you see some darker or lighter shades of gray strips that should be moved to another pile? Or snap a digital photo and upload it to your computer and view the image in black and white or grayscale on your computer screen.

- Another tool to use is a piece of red acetate, like a red, see-through report cover from an office supply store. Hold it between you and the fabric. The colors and their own peculiar assets are neutralized by the red, allowing you to see the values, not the colors.

- Quilt shops also stock value viewing tools.

each detail. To understand this, experiment with a flashlight and a mirror. Look in the mirror, then position the flashlight directly under your chin. Then move the flashlight to the left and notice what happens to the colors and shadows. Now hold it behind your head. Study what parts of your face become more accented as you move the light. What you're seeing are the affects of value (light and dark) on an object (your face).

Keep this hands-on lesson in mind when you compose a design. The location of the light source in your pattern will emphasize some objects more than others. Shadows and highlights or bright spots are hooked using extreme value changes to create a boundary between objects. This technique will also emphasize a layer.

HOW TO USE VALUE

To make the best use of your wool's values, put the following ideas to work in your designs.

♦ Dark backgrounds anchor and light backgrounds energize the design.

♦ Shadows are lack of light. If the object is round, a shadow will lighten at its outer edges. It will be darkest adjacent to the object. In dyeing for a shadow, select the complement of the object to dull the darker value.

♦ To suggest distance, use duller values/colors for the farthest away points.

♦ Bright, clear values/colors come to the foreground. Place them where the light source is hitting an object.

♦ Extreme changes in value between shapes will give more importance to the object, even if only used as an outline.

♦ Using value in a flat shape creates dimension, making a form.

■ EXERCISE #2 *Arranging Value*

LEARN: Choose three pieces of neutral wool from the brown or black families: light, medium, and dark. Pile them up in different ways: light on top, dark, medium on bottom; medium on top, just a thin amount of dark, then light on bottom; and so on. Keep playing around, showing more or less, one over the other. Photograph each version, or cut black, gray, and white pieces of paper and glue them in the same positions into your journal.

APPLY: Now choose five or six neutral wools or sheets of paper.

- Arrange them as if the sun is rising on a far ridgeline. Where would the brightest light hit? Place the lightest fabrics there.

- Now arrange them as if you were looking down an alleyway or through a tunnel. Where would the lightest and darkest pieces of wool be?

HOOK: Divide a 5" mat into nine squares. Select wool from one of your neutral brown or black families, in three different values: light, medium, and dark. In the middle square, use some of each of the fabrics. For each of the other squares, only use one fabric in each. You choose how many squares of each value. Now answer the following questions:

- Did you plan ahead to make this pattern? Or did you just take one fabric after the next?

- Which squares appear to advance and look like they are closer to you?

- What value would you choose to whip the edge?

- When the value you chose to whip the edge comes against itself in a square, how will the design be affected? Consider hooking a thin cut of color for the last row. I suggest you choose a medium value for this thin row.

- What would happen if the color was a textured wool with a lot of dark threads and in #6 cut? That might be less distracting than the solid medium color because of the variety of values in the textured wool. When you come against a dark square, the other values will be evident.

- Make another mat, changing the arrangements and how you hooked the center. Now ask the same questions and note how the answers change.

TEXTURE AND VALUE ■ 9

CHAPTER THREE

Line and Shape

"Everyone knows that even a single line may convey an emotion."
—Piet Mondrian (1872–1944)

Square: *Line, Neutrals,* 5" x 5", #8½-cut wool on linen. Designed and hooked by Devin Ryder, Cambridge, Massachusetts, 2010.

The next elements for us to study are line, shape, form, space, and scale. Consider these as foundation stones; they are the base on which the other elements are built.

LINE

The basic element is line. It is a joining of points along a surface. Individually or grouped, lines begin to activate a space, imply energy, or define boundaries. If you join a series of lines or close up a continuous line, you create a shape.

As rug hookers, our strips are our lines and the direction we hook them are the types of lines. We vary the width and achieve different effects by using solid or textured fabrics. Keep this concept in mind as you continue through the chapters.

STYLES OF LINES

Lines are either curved or straight. Curved lines are active, indicating movement. Linear or straight lines imply strength, and depending on position, may have potential for action. A vertical line might be stable, dignified, tall, or short: it might be a tree, fence, skyscraper, or a standing person. Horizontal lines imply calm, balance, and harmony. They define horizons, vistas, or a body at rest. Diagonal lines infer action: a plane taking off, an object thrown through the space, a person in motion—all of which are dramatic and energetic. Remember, we use lines as symbols to fool our mind. ▸

Square: *Line,* 5" x 5", #6-cut wool on linen. Designed and hooked by Jacqui Lee, E. Falmouth, Massachusetts, 2010.

		—	/
Tree	at rest	plane taking off
Stable, support	calm, balanced	action, energy
Building	horizon line	chaos
Person standing	road	person walking

EXERCISE #3 *Drawing Lines*

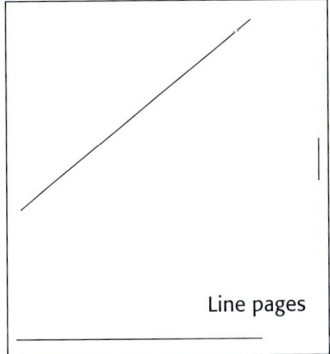

Line pages

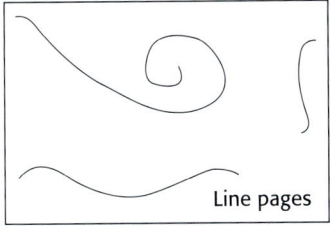

Line pages

LEARN: Take two blank pieces of paper, a pencil, and a ruler or straight edge. Fold each paper into four parts, then unfold. On one sheet, draw a straight line in each of three sections: one vertical, one horizontal, and one diagonal. On the second sheet, draw a curved line in the same three directions. In the fourth section of each sheet, in a few quick words, describe your reaction to the lines as they are positioned within the folded spaces. Your answers will be different depending on your own experiences. Remember, there are no wrong answers to this exercise.

Label these pages "Line," and place them in your journal or notebook.

HOOK: Get out your hooking tools, backing, and the kit of wools as suggested in chapter 1. Only use neutral fabrics for these first squares; however, select a range from light to dark.

Draw a 5" square on paper or directly on your backing, then add several lines incorporating both straight and curved, and short and long. (If you need to transfer your design from paper to your backing, see page 75 for instructions.) Look at what you drew. What story comes to mind? How can you accent this message with your different fabrics?

Use neutral wools for the first squares.

If nothing is coming to mind right away, don't fret. Forget the task for a while and cut some strips of fabric in a variety of widths. Keep your selection of fabrics simple, using only one fabric for the background.

ADVANCED: If you want to push yourself to be more creative, pick up one of your strips from the snarl pile at random and hook for a while. Then choose another, and hook it in a different part of the square. Once several lines have been "drawn" with your hooking, choose a fabric to complete each remaining space.

When you are finished, rotate your square by a quarter of a turn, then turn it again and again, considering your reactions each time.

- Can you tell stories about the different orientations? Does one position suggest a motif or a scene or a thought?
- Does the direction you hooked light fabrics enhance or diminish this tale?

Remember, directional hooking is a way of "drawing a line." Consider hooking a second mat reversing the background values and therefore also the value of each line. Did you emphasize other areas with these changes?

Square: *Line*

As you saw in the examples and your work, lines can *suggest* shapes, movement, depth or mass, and they can *imply* emotions or stories. Use lines with more consideration in your next project. Rather than pre-drawing Ss in your background, why not try organic freeform lines that will show more activity? Try this trick: use one unique strip of wool to lead the viewer's eye around your entire design.

LINE AND SHAPE ■ 11

Square: *Shape, Depth*

SHAPES

Shapes are created by joining lines. They are two-dimensional, with height and width. Each shape is defined by an edge. These boundaries allow us to distinguish an object from other shapes. Artists use other elements to emphasize one shape over another. These tools include value, color, and texture. Remember, the actual edges of your rug also create a shape.

We learn how to make simple shapes early in life: circles and ovals using curves; squares, rectangles or triangles using straight lines. How you arrange shapes is the next tool in our composition lesson.

Sensation, detail. (See the full rug on page 67)

Square: *Neutrals, Line,* 5" x 5", wool on linen. Designed and hooked by Peg Hartle, Woodville, Ontario, 2010.

Square: *Neutrals, Line*

■ EXERCISE #4 *Using Shapes*

LEARN: Fold a piece of paper or a journal page in four parts; open it up again. Select one of these three shapes: circle, square/rectangle, or triangle. Draw it in the first section. In section two, draw two different shapes of equal size. For the third section, compose a series of shapes showing movement or distance. In the fourth section, quickly describe in just a few words each of the three compositions. Put this paper in your journal and label it "Shapes."

APPLY: Review your drawings. In the first drawing, what size was the shape? Where did you put it within the folded section? Did you draw the full shape or put it in a corner of the page, with part of it spilling over the boundary? What would you call that shape: box, ball, orange . . . or is it a hole?

The second grouping tells more of a story because of the interaction between the two shapes and the background. Which shapes did you choose? What space did you give each object? If you rotate the page, do you see something different? Do you sense motion?

The third drawing tells the biggest story. How did you create movement? Did you change the sizes, use different shapes, overlap shapes, or draw some partially off the page?

HOOK: Back to the drawing board—either paper or backing. Draw two shapes and several lines, positioning them so there is action in the scene. Get out the neutral wools again and hook this square. When you're finished, answer the following questions:

- How did you fool the viewer into thinking the design has activity?
- Did you use different wools to emphasize a line?
- Are the lines straight or organic? What about the shapes?
- Did you overlap objects and use light fabric for the one on top?
- Is a shape sitting on the edge or on a line?

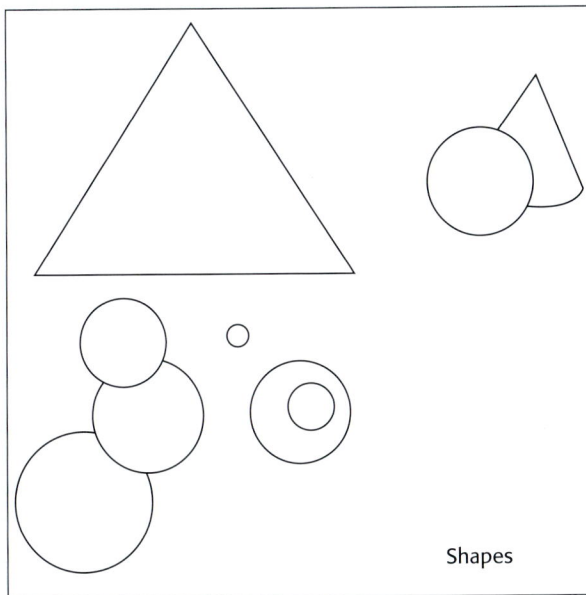

Shapes

LINE AND SHAPE ■ 13

CHAPTER FOUR

Form, Space, and Scale

"When the color is at its richest, form is at its fullest."
—Paul Cezanne (1839–1906)

Red barns against a green landscape and blue sky offer an excellent opportunity to study shape.

Everyday life, such as a set table, is a study in shapes.

A three-dimensional object has form. Three-dimensional forms can be measured: from top to bottom (height), side to side (width), and from back to front (depth). Two other elements, space and value, help to determine form, and the amount of light on any part of a shape will determine the viewer's visual perception of form. We recognize two types of form: geometric shapes, like a box; and natural shapes, like a flower petal.

Form may be created by combining two or more shapes. It may be enhanced by value, texture, and color. In rug hooking, most of our pieces are flat, so we work with implied dimension, although our many techniques can enhance actual depth.

14

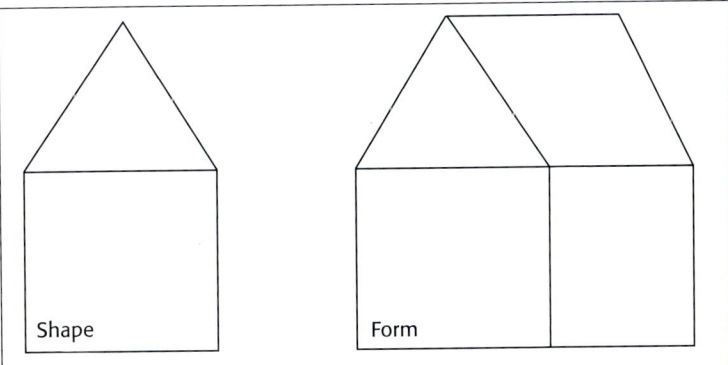

Simple perspective is achieved in the drawing on the right by connecting two more shapes to the simple sketch. The new design is familiar to our eyes as a side view of a building. Selecting one side to be lighter will emphasize depth.

Square: *Form*

The Cutting Garden, detail. (See the full rug on page 67.)

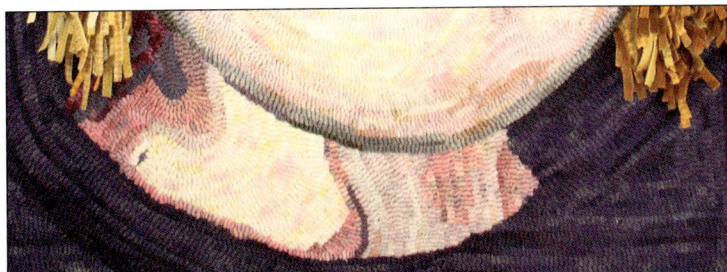

Lindsey, detail. (See the full rug on page 65.) Shading gives dimension to the chin.

Coming Into Town, detail. (See the full rug on page 69.)

Here are some simple tricks to add depth to an object. One trick is to hook one or more rows of a slightly different value halfway around the shape. Or you can create a shadow by using a different shade of fabric hooked as an elongated shape angled away from the object. Folk artists portray building dimensions by coloring the side away from light dark; the side facing the light is lighter. Primitive designs usually use blocks of color, outlining, or a change of value to convey form. The more complicated or detailed an artist uses materials and techniques, the more a form becomes lifelike. This is true in any medium.

FORM, SPACE, AND SCALE ■ **15**

The ridgeline and fence posts in this photo give the appearance of distance.

A stand at a farmer's market in Holland, Michigan, is a feast for the eyes. Notice the shapes, forms, and spaces.

The March, detail. (See the full rug on page 46.)

Square: *Space*

Square: *Tree Space*

SPACE

Every shape takes up **space**. Space refers to the distances or areas around, between, or within components of a design. The outside dimensions of your rug define its space.

We use two types of space in artistic composition: positive and negative. **Positive space** refers to the area a shape takes up. **Negative space** refers to the space around and between those shapes. We add layers with either horizontal lines or layered objects, creating different planes of activity—foreground, middle ground, and background.

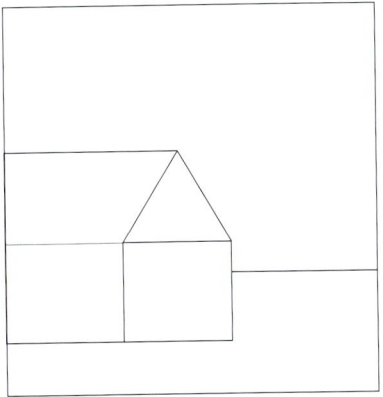 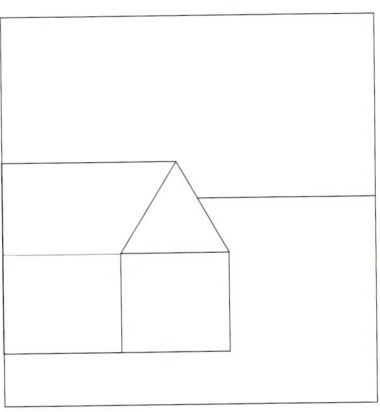 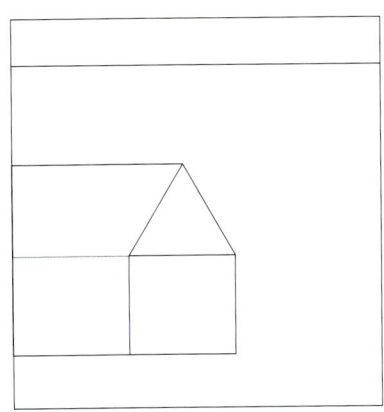

In these three diagrams, I moved the horizon line. How does changing the space around the object affect your perception of it? What if more lines were added—curves for hills or lines angled to represent a road?

Island Sunrise, detail. (See the full rug on page 44.)

■ EXERCISE #5 *Adding Dimension*

Square: *Form*

Square: *Perspective*

HOOK: Draw a simple shape or series of shapes, adding dimension to at least one with connected shapes. Continue to use neutral wools and hook this square. Select fabrics that will allow you to depict a shadow or a light source on the objects. Keep in mind that the background value will enhance the effect.

FORM, SPACE, AND SCALE ■ 17

Square: *Form, Scale*

Hillside, detail. (See the full rug on page 49.)

A bowl of tomatoes is a study of scale and form.

SCALE

Scale is the relationship of one object to other objects, and it is tied into how space is used. You can create importance in a composition by exaggerating scale, making one element much larger or smaller than all the rest. Georgia O'Keefe's large paintings of close-up floral details are good examples of scale. The Canadian collective of artists known as The Group of Seven used scale to communicate the vast natural resources of Canada.

Books and the Internet help you understand this concept, but visiting original art gives the full sense of scale the artist wanted to portray. I walked into the exhibit space at the National Gallery in Ottawa where The Group of Seven's gigantic canvases hung with plenty of space around each, and I was overwhelmed.

■ EXERCISE #6 *Showing Depth*

LEARN: Focus on how space, both negative and positive, affects your perception of a design.

APPLY: Draw several versions of a design, incorporating a road and hills. In one version, make the road very important to the viewer. In another, create a busy background.

HOOK: Draw a square on your backing. Inside it, design a landscape with depth. Hook it, once again using only neutral fabrics, or one color with a full range from light to dark.

18 ■ DESIGN BASICS FOR RUG HOOKERS

CHAPTER FIVE

Color

"I found I could say things with color and shapes that I couldn't say in any other way—things that I had no words for." —Georgia O'Keefe (1887–1986)

Colour Theory, detail. Ingrid Hieronimus, Ontario, Canada.

Collect samples to help you understand and choose colors for your projects.

Most of us are intimidated by the thought of entering the mysterious world of color. This chapter will help you break it down into small parts, easier to explore.

Understanding some terminology will be helpful. Color is light reflecting off surfaces that absorb parts of the waves and reflect others; the reflected pieces are perceived by our eyes as color. Isaac Newton in 1676 proved that light was made up of colored wavelengths by passing it through two prisms. To diagram this, he bent the spectrum into a circle, or color wheel, that we use to this day. Other artists configure colors in a variety of shapes, including squares or triangles. Most of us have become familiar with the basic form of a wheel with six main sections: red, orange, yellow, green, blue, violet.

People react to colors emotionally. As I said before, life experiences will affect each individual's response to a rug. As a teenager, my brother was comfortable in a very dark red bedroom, while I chose medium pea green. (Can you figure out what decade that was?) Psychological studies have found blood pressures change when people are in rooms of different colors, advertising campaigns succeed or fail because of packaging and color, and of course, society places meaning on color: white dresses for weddings in the West and red dresses in the East; boys in blue and girls in pink. ▸

PF Colours, detail. (See the full rug on page 50.)

Red Flower Geometric Study. Shades of red and its complement, green.

Blue Flower Geometric Study. Shades of blue and its complement, orange.

process makes shades. Red with its complement green added would become maroon.

A color appears lighter when surrounded by very dark colors or black. It appears darker when it is surrounded by a very light color or white. And the same colored wool will appear dull when similar valued wools are hooked around it. Consider these principles when you choose the value of the background or motifs for your next rug.

Every color (hue) has a particular value based on light reflectance. An easy way to understand this is to think about how complements react to each other. We can use the mathematical ratios to our advantage. The primary complement pairs' ratios are yellow to violet, 1:3; blue to orange, 1:2; and red to green, equal at 1:1. In other words, you need three times the amount of violet to tone down a yellow, but you can have half of

the design in red and the other half in green and be bored, unless you also used bright and dark values.

Monochromatic

A **monochromatic** palette has variations in value and intensity within a single hue. This palette uses different tints and shades of one color, such as we see when we move from pink to rose to red to maroon. A design with one hue can be very dramatic depending on how you use value and contrast.

Temperature

Warm colors are made up of yellow and red pigments, while cool colors incorporate blue. There can be a cool red and a warm blue, depending on the amount of the other primary in the color.

CHAPTER FIVE

Color

"I found I could say things with color and shapes that I couldn't say in any other way—things that I had no words for." —Georgia O'Keefe (1887–1986)

Colour Theory, detail. Ingrid Hieronimus, Ontario, Canada.

Collect samples to help you understand and choose colors for your projects.

Most of us are intimidated by the thought of entering the mysterious world of color. This chapter will help you break it down into small parts, easier to explore.

Understanding some terminology will be helpful. Color is light reflecting off surfaces that absorb parts of the waves and reflect others; the reflected pieces are perceived by our eyes as color. Isaac Newton in 1676 proved that light was made up of colored wavelengths by passing it through two prisms. To diagram this, he bent the spectrum into a circle, or color wheel, that we use to this day. Other artists configure colors in a variety of shapes, including squares or triangles. Most of us have become familiar with the basic form of a wheel with six main sections: red, orange, yellow, green, blue, violet.

People react to colors emotionally. As I said before, life experiences will affect each individual's response to a rug. As a teenager, my brother was comfortable in a very dark red bedroom, while I chose medium pea green. (Can you figure out what decade that was?) Psychological studies have found blood pressures change when people are in rooms of different colors, advertising campaigns succeed or fail because of packaging and color, and of course, society places meaning on color: white dresses for weddings in the West and red dresses in the East; boys in blue and girls in pink. ▶

SECTION TWO • THE ELEMENTS

■ EXERCISE #7 *Reacting to Color*

LEARN: Use this experiment to help you understand the effects of value and textures on a color.

APPLY: Cut a 2" square of colored paper and place it on several of your other colored papers—white, black, colored, even patterned scrapbooking papers. Observe how the square changes based on its environment. Do different background colors create changes in feeling or effect?

HOOK: Divide a hooking square into four parts. Draw a shape in each section, then hook the shapes with one wool fabric. Now complete each section with black (very dark) in one square, white (natural) in the second square, a medium texture in the third, and the original color's opposite (complement) in the last square. Look back at your paper swatches: does the wool react the same as the paper?

Leaf Peeping Season, detail. (See the full rug on page 60.)

COLOR TERMINOLOGY

We have many color terms. They all help us communicate clearly with each other about color and its properties. Let's define each one.

Intensity

Intensity refers to the quality of light in a color. (This is quality—not quantity. The quantity of light is the value.) Intensity means the brightness or dullness of the same hue. For example, think about looking at a landscape. The mountains or objects farthest appear hazy, washed out in color. They are less intense. The moisture in the atmosphere softens the colors. A color is most intense in its purest form; you can dull a color by adding gray or, in dyeing, by adding its complement.

▶ **TIP:** Use intensity to emphasize an object. You can draw attention to a motif even if it is smaller than the others. For example, if you use a color that is dull in intensity, an object will appear farther away even if the other objects are the same color.

UNDERSTANDING INTENSITY

When using the terms value and intensity, think of the common rug hooking phrase: light, bright, dark, and dull.

Eric Sandberg has provided the following recipes to dip dye around the color wheel with all four of the light, bright, dark, and dull characteristics.

Note: Each recipe line is two separate recipes. Make the first part, dip the wool, then make the second recipe and complete the transition. Read the instructions below before beginning.

Eric Sandberg's light, bright, dark, and dull

RECIPES FOR LIGHT, BRIGHT, DARK, AND DULL AROUND THE COLOR WHEEL

RED	1/4 t 338 in 1 CBW add to dye bath and dip wool until clear. Then make the second color using 3/8 t 119 + 1/8 490 in 1 CBW. Add this color to same dye bath return wool, dippping as instructed.
RED-ORANGE	3/16 t 338 + 1/8 t 119 as in first part of RED formula then 3/16 t 119 + 3/32 t 490 for second color
ORANGE	1/8 t 338 + 3/8 t 119 then 1/16 t 490
YELLOW-ORANGE	1/16 t 338 + 3/8 t 119 then 3/64 t 338 + 1/32 t 490
YELLOW	3/8 t 119 then 3/128 t 338 + 1/64 t 490
YELLOW-GREEN	3/8 t 119 + 1/32 t 490 then 3/128 t 338 + 1/64 t 490
GREEN	3/8 t 119 + 1/16 t 490 then 1/16 t 338
BLUE-GREEN	3/64 t 119 + 3/32 t 490 then 1/16 t 119 + 1/16 t 338
BLUE	1/8 t 490 then 3/8 t 119 + 1/8 t 338
BLUE-VIOLET	3/32 t 490 + 1/8 t 338 then 3/16 t 119 + 1/16 t 338
VIOLET	1/16 t 490 + 1/8 t 338 then 1/8 t 119
RED-VIOLET	1/32 t 490 + 1/8 t 338 then 1/8 t 119 + 1/64 t 490

Use Pro-Chem Wash Fast Acid Dyes:
- 119 Yellow
- 338 Magenta
- 490 Blue

t = teaspoon

1CBW = one cup boiling water

Instructions: Put the first color of each recipe into a pot with vinegar or citric acid already in the heated water. Dip three quarters of a 24" x 30" strip of wool (natural, white, or neutral texture) up and down. Near the end of color in the bath, dip the full piece to give it this slight color, taking up the balance of dye in the pan. Your piece is now "bright and light." Then pour the second part of recipe in the dye bath, adding water and acid if necessary. Take the same strip of dyed wool and put the bright end into pot. Dip up to half of the strip, clearing the bath. Your piece now transitions from "light and bright" to "dark and dull."

Squares: *Complements*

Squares: *Complements*

Squares: *Monochromatic*

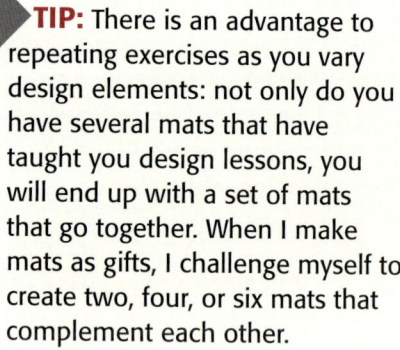

TIP: There is an advantage to repeating exercises as you vary design elements: not only do you have several mats that have taught you design lessons, you will end up with a set of mats that go together. When I make mats as gifts, I challenge myself to create two, four, or six mats that complement each other.

Primary

Only three colors are considered pure, that is, without other colors. They are the three **primary colors**: red, yellow, and blue. Ingrid Hieronimus has created a full color wheel including value swatches for each color in her book, *Primary Fusion*. She uses Pro-Chemical Wash Fast Acid Dyes, 119 Yellow, 338 Magenta, 490 Blue, and 672 Black.

Secondary

From these three colors we can make three more secondary, or complementary, colors by mixing equal parts of two primaries. The complement of red is green (mix blue and yellow). Yellow's complement is violet (red and blue). And the opposite of blue is orange (red and yellow).

Square: *Color, Primary*

22 ■ DESIGN BASICS FOR RUG HOOKERS

Values: light, medium, and dark.

Square: *Stink Bug Study.* Intense and light values advance and dark values recede.

Look at a color wheel. The three complementary colors are located directly opposite the primary colors. In dyeing, introducing the complement to a dye bath will make the existing wool dull or antiqued. Eventually, if you add enough of the complementary color, the wool will become brown or muddied. Each combination creates a unique brown.

Tertiary

Tertiary colors are made by mixing equal amounts of a primary color and a secondary color. Red and orange make red-orange. But if there is more yellow with the orange it is yellow-orange and so on around the wheel.

Analogous

Think of **analogous** colors as friendly neighbors. They appear next to each other on the wheel. Using three analogous colors in a rug is comfortable. They create the feeling of balance and unity—they belong together.

If you wanted to create tension or excitement, select a color and the two colors next to its complement. This pairing is

Rider and Friend, detail. (See the full rug on page 56.)

called a split complement. We already know that complements used in equal amounts merge, or dilute each other. Analogous color combinations are appealing.

Rainbow of Trees, detail. (See the full rug on page 60.)

Hue

Hue is the name given to a color family. The hues in the spectrum are red, orange, yellow, green, blue, and violet.

We explored value with respect to light and darkness. We can also apply that concept to any hue. Consider that reds range from light red to dark red, from pale pink to deep maroon.

In dyeing, we add increments of the same dye formula to darken a piece of wool without changing its hue. This process creates a tint. For example, red lightened becomes pink. If we added increments of the hue immediately opposite the color, we would dull the original color, eventually approaching brown. This

COLOR ■ 23

PF Colours, detail. (See the full rug on page 50.)

Red Flower Geometric Study. Shades of red and its complement, green.

Blue Flower Geometric Study. Shades of blue and its complement, orange.

process makes shades. Red with its complement green added would become maroon.

A color appears lighter when surrounded by very dark colors or black. It appears darker when it is surrounded by a very light color or white. And the same colored wool will appear dull when similar valued wools are hooked around it. Consider these principles when you choose the value of the background or motifs for your next rug.

Every color (hue) has a particular value based on light reflectance. An easy way to understand this is to think about how complements react to each other. We can use the mathematical ratios to our advantage. The primary complement pairs' ratios are yellow to violet, 1:3; blue to orange, 1:2; and red to green, equal at 1:1. In other words, you need three times the amount of violet to tone down a yellow, but you can have half of

the design in red and the other half in green and be bored, unless you also used bright and dark values.

Monochromatic

A **monochromatic** palette has variations in value and intensity within a single hue. This palette uses different tints and shades of one color, such as we see when we move from pink to rose to red to maroon. A design with one hue can be very dramatic depending on how you use value and contrast.

Temperature

Warm colors are made up of yellow and red pigments, while cool colors incorporate blue. There can be a cool red and a warm blue, depending on the amount of the other primary in the color.

Mile Marker 62, 8" x 10", #5- and 6-cut wool on monk's cloth. Designed and hooked by Susan Feller, Augusta, West Virginia, 2010.

Color palette from nature

Square: *Color, Warm*

Dorr color value swatches

COLOR TOOLS

Use these color tools when you are planning a design:

- Warm colors seem to advance while cool colors recede.
- Using bright or intense colors in large spaces will make that area advance.
- The reverse is true: dark and dull colors appear to recede.
- Harmonious effects can be achieved by selecting colors next to each other on the color wheel.
- If you used warm and cool colors in the same piece there will be tension; all warm or all cool is calming.
- Use the color wheel as a tool, not a crutch. It is a visual way to verify a specific color when talking to someone else. You and I may understand green differently—my green could be closer to yellow than your green.
- Names of colors are personal, and colors are a big business. Think of the new names that come out each season in the fashion and decorating worlds.
- Color is emotional.
- Learn about the effect of colors on other colors by experimenting.
- Where will the rug be exhibited? In a bright room? Choose more intense values than if the rug is displayed in a darker room.
- Light values in a dark space used sparingly will enhance medium values.
- Repeat the mantra: Light, bright, dark, and dull. Ask yourself: Do I have them all in this rug? Are they in a pleasing proportion? Do they tell the story?

CHAPTER SIX

Pattern, Contrast, and Emphasis

"If I could have had my own way, I would have confined myself to black and white." —Edgar Degas, 1834–1917

Floral Color Study, detail. (See the full rug on page 58.)

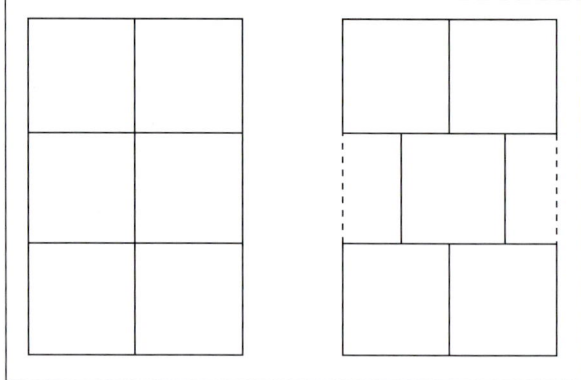

Block pattern (left) and brick or half-drop pattern (right).

Pattern is defined as a single unit of design used in repetition. This can be a shape or line, arranged in such a manner as to evoke texture, convey movement, allude to depth, or create a border or resting spot in the design. You'll find repeat patterns in home furnishings, textiles, floor, and wall coverings. Nature is filled with repeated patterns. The basic domestic crafts use patterning, and when enhanced by color, value, or texture, crafts become decorative and artistic. Think of the patterns in weaving, coiled pottery, quilting stitches, and basket making.

If you duplicate a shape in one row, you create a band or border. You can repeat a pattern over an entire surface to make a design. Randomly placed and repeated elements also create a pattern.

PLANNED PATTERNS

Two basic layouts are used in the design industry to construct **planned patterns**. They are block patterns and brick patterns.

A **block** composition is a grid of horizontal and vertical lines. Nola Heidbreder's *Floral Color Study* uses the block pattern arrangement, repeating the same flower shape within a very visible grid. If she had chosen to use just the light gray and eliminated the background colors in each square, the arrangement would still be block, but the flowers would seem to be floating. You can vary the arrangement by positioning the grid on the diagonal, but the blocks are still stacked directly above and side by side. Shirley Winklepleck's diamond motif (*page 27*) exemplifies this block format.

Brick layouts involve rows of alternating positions. This is also called half drop, as the pattern is created by moving the shape one half of the width of

▶ **TIP:** Rug shows are often set up by category. Study the geometric rug designs in a show to identify patterns, repeats, and how changes in scale, value, color, and texture affect the emphasis.

Old Traditional Pattern, detail. (See the full rug on page 57.) This is a block pattern.

Diamonds, detail. (See the full rug on page 55.) This is a block pattern.

Maggie's Penny Runner, detail. (See the full rug on page 66.) This is a half-drop pattern.

PATTERN, CONTRAST, AND EMPHASIS ■ 27

Her Favorite Red Shoes, detail. (See the full rug on page 43.)

Papal Squares, detail. (See the full rug on page 57.)

Spontaneous arrangements using the same object create active patterns.

the object to the right with each row. Coloring a brick pattern in a set pattern creates a rhythm. The border of *Maggie's Penny Runner* (*page 27*) uses a common half moon shape, or lamb's tongue, repeated in this manner.

RANDOM PATTERNS

A **random pattern**, when an element is repeated in unusual ways, adds interest to a design. The proportion, color, value, or materials may change, directing your attention to a focal point or moving it around. Ellen Banker repeated a circle motif in her border and the shoes in a random pattern (*Her Favorite Red Shoes,* above left). She implied dimension to the shoes by positioning dots on the "sides." The partial circles at the edge of her border imply activity and whimsy. To emphasize the shape even more, she hooked lines of bright green around the circles in the border.

28 ■ DESIGN BASICS FOR RUG HOOKERS

■ EXERCISE #8 *Repeating Pattern*

Squares: *Planned Pattern, Movement*

LEARN: Now you will create a repeated pattern. Choose a style—block, brick, or random—and draw it inside a square.

HOOK: Sort your scrap bag into color families. Take one of these bundles and hook your design. Then using the same composition, change the color, the value, or the background fabric. How does this change affect the design?

Random patterns are visible in everyday life, such as those seen in this facade.

PATTERNS IN EVERYDAY LIFE

Throughout history, artists have used animals, figures, florals, scenic vignettes, geometrics, and textures in repeated patterns. Pieced quilt blocks are a great source of patterns. Look through home furnishings catalogs or websites and locate both planned and random patterns. What types of shapes are commonly repeated?

Where can you find planned and random patterns in your everyday life? The supermarket shelves are excellent resources for study. Instead of shopping, roam the store with a journal. Write down your feelings and make sketches. How do you feel as you enter different aisles? Look closely at the shelves, then sketch the shelving pattern. The scale of objects, colors, shapes of containers, and empty spaces all excite our senses. Draw the pattern of shelved cereal boxes and then the horizontal packages of cookies.

How have produce managers created patterns with the fruits and vegetables? During the summer, I enjoy visiting local farmers' markets. Artful displays entice me and are subjects for future rug designs.

Look beyond your feet when you are touring churches and museums. Do you see patterns in parquetry woods or mosaic floors? The patterned facades on buildings along the streets draw our attention to an entrance or sign.

CONTRAST

Contrast provides visual interest. As we now know, all of the elements have wide ranges. To draw attention toward a motif, we know we should surround it with a color, value, shape, direction of hooking, or texture from the opposite range. Extreme examples of contrasts might be intense yellow teamed up with dull, dark violet; white and black; a large round sphere with a skinny triangular shadow; or a thin line suggesting a shape as in Judy Privett's *Sensation* (page 67).

Jigsaw Rabbit (page 30) has great contrast. Consider the ways your interest is piqued. I immediately see a large, bright, organic-shaped leaping rabbit. The

Study repeating patterns when you see them around you, such as this one at the farmer's market in Holland, Michigan.

PATTERN, CONTRAST, AND EMPHASIS ■ 29

Jigsaw Rabbit, 8" x 16", #5-cut wool on linen. Designed and hooked by Nancy Jewett, Salisbury, Vermont, 2008.

unusual puzzle pieces she chose as the background make me smile. How would the action be affected if the shapes were geometric or if she had hooked a landscape in the background? What if the rabbit were outlined with a thin dark green like she used in the border? This treatment would make the animal more prominent, but because she used a subtle range of values in the hues, she kept a light, airy feeling to the design. The attention-getting yellow pieces are evenly distributed to accent the leaping animal. Jewett used an equal amount of warm and cool solid colors in the background, effectively keeping our attention on the central motif. To frame the design Nancy chose the complementary pair that produces the least contrast: red and green. However, the border values are the darkest and therefore contain and anchor the flying rabbit.

Look at the same rug in grayscale. The lightest value by far is the central motif. Nancy used a solid dark green to portray the distant valley. It was an extreme jump in value from the lightly mottled rabbit.

30 ■ DESIGN BASICS FOR RUG HOOKERS

▶ **TIP:** When a shadow is needed, determine the complement of the color you are using. Mix this hue into the color of the motif to make a realistic shadow. For example, a shadow behind a yellow tulip should include a bit of violet.

Even though the edges of this shadow are uneven, the value changes identify the shape.

Coming Into Town, detail. (See the full rug on page 69.)

■ EXERCISE #9 *Emphasizing Contrast*

LEARN: Choose one of the following elements to create a square with contrast.

- Value (light and dark). Draw a shape. Use extreme values for the shape and the background.
- Color. Use bright hues in the area you want the viewer to notice, and dark or dull colors for the other spaces.
- Texture. Include prodding or some other fiber technique in the design.

HOOK: Hook the design with your selections of wool and techniques. To complete the lesson, reverse the materials and/or techniques and make a second mat. Evaluate how the two are different. Which one portrays contrast the best? Now you have two samples, and you also have a set. Pairs are great gifts and are useful in decorating.

PATTERN, CONTRAST, AND EMPHASIS ■ 31

Peace on Earth, detail. (See the full rug on page 62.)

EMPHASIS

Emphasis refers to areas of interest that guide the viewers' eyes into and out of the image.

Emphasis or dominance of an object can be increased by making the object larger, more sophisticated, or more ornate; by placing it in the foreground; or by making it stand out visually more than any other object in a piece by using color or value. Selecting a limited color palette might emphasize a particular mood.

Plan your rug with the primary focal point in mind. That is the area which should receive the largest emphasis, drawing the most attention. The main motif in Christine Walker-Bird's *Double Pots* is simplified in scale and repeated in the border. The message of *Peace on Earth* is emphasized by repeating the houses, placing them evenly on the round earth.

Double Pots, detail. (See the full rug on page 50.)

32 ■ DESIGN BASICS FOR RUG HOOKERS

CHAPTER SEVEN

Rhythm and Movement

"Art makes order out of chaos." —Stephen Sondheim (1930–)

Square: *Square Log Cabin,* 6" square on linen. Designed and hooked by Peg Hartle, Woodville, Ontario, 2010.

Flowing rhythm is demonstrated with this display of Glaceau Vitamin Water.

We feel rhythm in music: the pulsing beat of an island drum or the flowing sound of instruments chiming in on a familiar chorus. Visual rhythm is achieved in the same way—repeating a shape, color, or line in a regular pattern.

Movement is action. We see action play out everyday in our towns and cities as we watch cars and people go about their daily work. In our backyards, we see the trees sway in the wind and the animals scurrying about.

In this chapter, we'll take a look at how to portray rhythm and movement in a static hooked rug.

Movement is implied in this hall runner by the angled lines of contrasting color.

RHYTHM

Rhythm as a principle is used to organize a composition and create interest, unity, or emphasis. We will consider three styles of rhythm: regular, flowing, and alternating.

Regular rhythm is made up of equal shapes that are balanced and continue throughout the design. The pattern is not interrupted. In music, this would be the drumbeat of a march cadence. ▶

SECTION THREE • THE PRINCIPLES

LEFT: *Sea Creatures,* detail. (See the full rug on page 40.)

BELOW: *Let the River Run,* detail. (See the full rug on page 48.)

BOTTOM: *Yellow Pot,* detail. (See the full rug on page 56.)

Believe in Yourself, detail. (See the full rug on page 1.)

Flowing rhythm is created by placing objects along an imaginary curve. Gradual changes of value from form to form in such a composition can accent the gentle feeling of a flowing rhythm. Think of water moving, air currents, tumbling shapes—all flow undisturbed in synchronization.

A musical equivalent to alternating rhythm in a rug is jazz. Some element ties the composition together, but the work has an upbeat or discordant mood. Bright colors, bold angular shapes, and asymmetry could build an alternating rhythm.

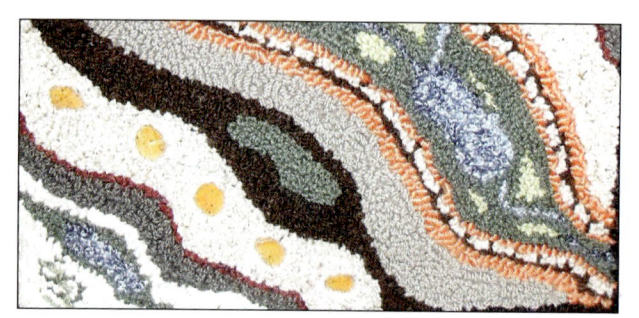

34 ■ DESIGN BASICS FOR RUG HOOKERS

A selection of dyed wools shimmers with color and rhythm.

Motion can be achieved with a consistent directional line or lines. Many thin, long lines arranged close together will look active. Bending straight lines in a grid can imply tension and the feeling that the lines or objects are moving apart.

Where we place an object to imply movement will help us see it in motion. In your journal, draw a road on an angle and place a car disappearing off the page. Do you perceive the motion? What other scenarios would imply similar movement? Remember, we are playing with the viewer's mind; the goal is to make him or her think action is happening in our static design.

Try layering shapes in uneven spacing and changing the values or colors to suggest that a pile is falling apart, creating a feeling of chaos. If you spaced the motifs evenly and used a regular gradation of values, the viewer sees the composition as static. If you introduce rhythm, the viewer sees motion.

Square: *Rhythm*

Square: *Movement*

RHYTHM AND MOVEMENT ■ 35

CHAPTER EIGHT

Balance and Unity

"When I haven't any blue I use red."
"Why do two colors, put one next to the other, sing?
Can one really explain this? No."
—Pablo Picasso (1881–1973)

Square: *Owl*

This image of trapped ice bubbles streaming from the center of the bowl is an example of a radial design.

You choose your rug design based on the purpose of the project. Is the work going to be a rug on the floor or will it hang on the wall? Decorative elements and motifs change with the viewing angle, environment, light, and attitude of the viewer. Be sure to consider these as you choose your pattern or design. Take the time to occasionally view the piece in its intended position as you work on it. Throw it on the floor and walk around it, or tack it to a wall and stand across the room. This quick check will tell you if the piece is working as you had planned.

BALANCE

Balance can be symmetrical, asymmetrical, or radial. **Symmetry** is achieved when equal shapes and weights are placed opposite each other. This type of design runs the risk of being boring. But if you add slight changes to disrupt the symmetry, you will most likely be pleased with the effect. Informal balance, or **asymmetry**, happens when an energetic shape is countered with a passive shape, but the coloring, size, or direction of the energy line is similar. **Radial balance** is where equal parts radiate from a central element, like a sunflower's rings of seeds curving progressively outwards.

Balance can be achieved by the location of objects, volume or sizes of objects, and by color. It can also be achieved by balancing lighter colors with darker colors or bold colors with light neutral colors.

The key to achieving balance lies in perception. The eye perceives weights being equal and balanced when the objects that hold those weights have the same value or intensity of color and create harmony. Look at the inner panel of *Maggie's Penny Runner* on page 66. ▶

SECTION THREE • THE PRINCIPLES

36

■ EXERCISE #10 *Balancing Motifs*

LEARN: A common design technique to create balance in a piece of art is to place motifs of equal size along an imaginary triangle, circle, or square.

APPLY: Place a journal page vertically in front of you and sketch a box approximately 5" square. Choose your favorite shape—this will become your "invisible" trail. Using a four-petal flower shape, draw a balanced bouquet following your invisible trail. If you change your invisible shape, how many motifs do you need to imply the new shape?

HOOK: Create a balanced bouquet in a container to hook in a 5" square.

No. 2 Pencils, detail. (See the full rug on page 61.)

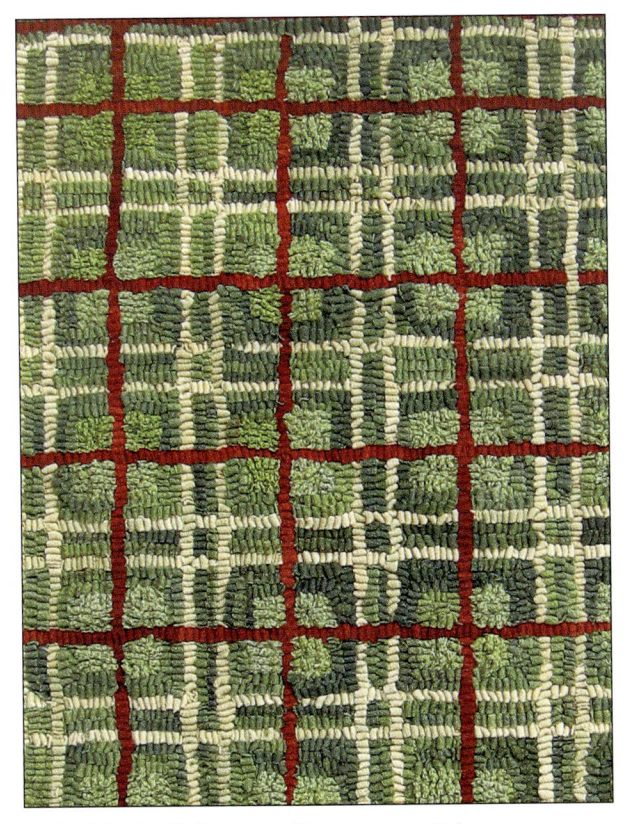

Bev's Plaid, detail. (See the full rug on page 62.)

UNITY

Unity refers to a sense that everything in a piece of work belongs there and contributes to the whole design. Repetition, balance of shapes in a mirrored effect, harmonious color, and value all unify. A work should feel complete—as if nothing can be added or taken away. Look at *PF Colors* on page 50.

It is a challenge for rug hookers to create a composition that has variety yet feels complete, or unified. Consider these tips:

- ◆ Design: Is there one line or shape, either visible or implied, which pulls the piece together? In other words, did you arrange the motifs in a repeat of the prominent shape?
- ◆ Color: Consider using a wide range of values in one hue. This monochromatic color plan will unify your design.
- ◆ Value: Background values should unify the entire piece. Have you used the background value in small amounts in the motifs? If you do, your rug will have more depth and balance.
- ◆ Texture: Try using a particular texture in a variety of colors throughout the design. It is a subtle touch that the viewer's eye will pick out and this small touch will add to the unity of the piece.

BALANCE AND UNITY ■ 37

Walking in Old Montreal, detail. (See the full rug on page 42.)

Spirit Dance, detail. (See the full rug on page 48.)

▶ Negative Space is a Plus

When you look at a design, consider the space around each shape, the background that we call negative space. Learn to look beyond the objects in a design and use that space to your advantage. When we use the background as another design element, we unify and balance the entire piece.

Advertising campaigns use all space to communicate. For example, consider FedEx. Look at the negative space in this logo. Do you see the arrow? It is between the E and the X, pointing you forward, adding movement to the design.

38 ■ DESIGN BASICS FOR RUG HOOKERS

CHAPTER NINE

Gallery of Rugs

Take a look at the hooked pieces portrayed in these pages.
The bold words at the end of each caption identify elements
or principles illustrated in the piece.
See if you recognize other elements and principles.
Analyze each rug to determine the artist's message.

SCALE

CONTRAST

EMPHASIS

PATTERN

BALANCE

SECTION FOUR • THE GALLERY

Three Elements of Design, 18" x 38", #6-cut and proddy wool on linen. Designed and hooked by Mary Jane Peabody, Wilmot, New Hampshire, 2010. IMPACT XPOZURES

    Mary Jane has done a series of rugs based on doodles. She's talked to many people who say, "Oh, I can't draw," but every single person had one or two ways of doodling. Mary Jane said, "I'm convinced it's a good way to loosen up people who say they couldn't ever make their own design."

LINE, COLOR, TEXTURE, PATTERN, UNITY

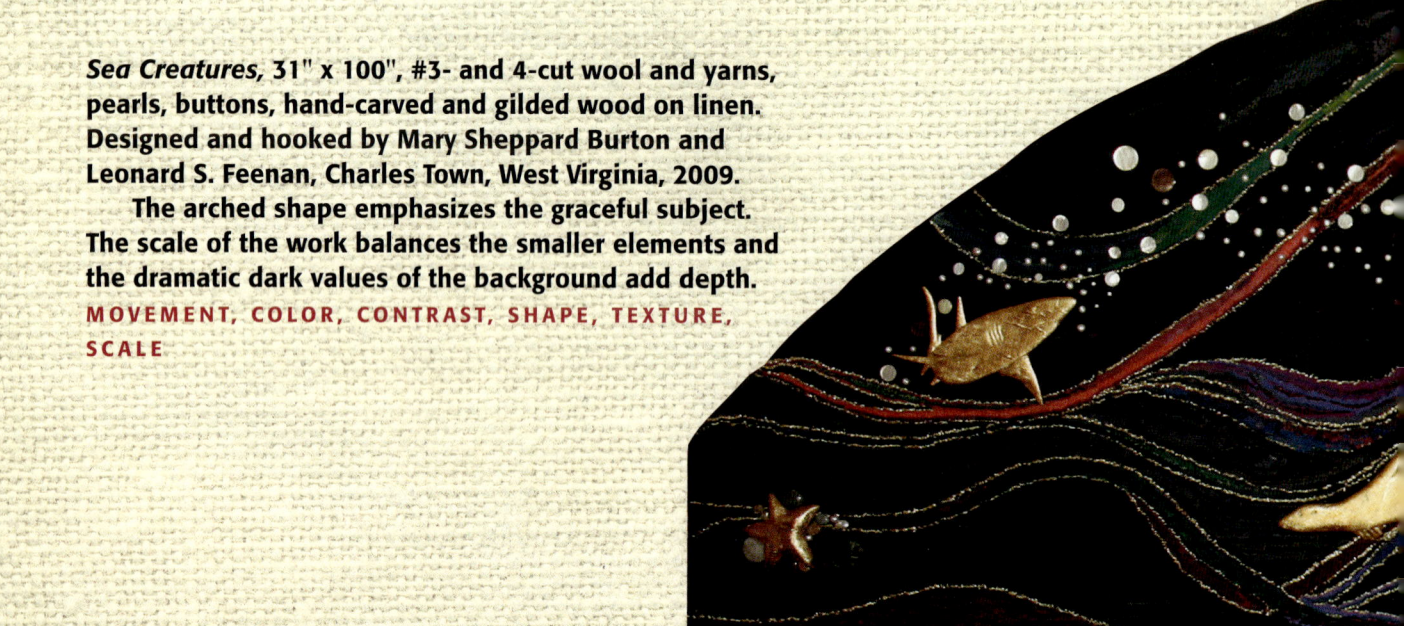

Sea Creatures, 31" x 100", #3- and 4-cut wool and yarns, pearls, buttons, hand-carved and gilded wood on linen. Designed and hooked by Mary Sheppard Burton and Leonard S. Feenan, Charles Town, West Virginia, 2009.

    The arched shape emphasizes the graceful subject. The scale of the work balances the smaller elements and the dramatic dark values of the background add depth.

MOVEMENT, COLOR, CONTRAST, SHAPE, TEXTURE, SCALE

40 ■ DESIGN BASICS FOR RUG HOOKERS

A Perfect World, 17 ½", #3-, 4-, and 5-cut wool on monk's cloth. Designed and hooked by Mariah Krauss, Montpelier, Vermont, 2009.

Four years of studying in faraway Montana emphasized the importance of home and friends for Mariah. This composition tells a story in words and symbols; her use of neutral black and white for the background unifies these two. **PATTERN, SCALE, CONTRAST, RHYTHM**

GALLERY OF RUGS ■ 41

Waiting in Old Montreal, 15" x 23", #3- and 4-cut wool on rug warp. Designed and hooked by Stephanie Allen-Krauss, Montpelier, Vermont, 2010.

Texture, value changes, careful sizing of the buildings, and the positions of the walkers all help to draw the viewer down the street. The subtle palette complements the old feeling of the subject. SCALE, SPACE, UNITY, VALUE

Grenfell Goose, 10 1/2", #4-cut wool and hand-dyed nylon stockings on burlap. Designed and hooked by Stephanie Ashworth-Krauss, Montpelier, Vermont, 1995.

Hooked in horizontal rows to mimic the Grenfell style, the large central figure is flying because of the position of the wings and the lower horizon line. SCALE, COLOR, MOVEMENT, CONTRAST

Her Favorite Red Shoes, 28½" x 27½", #4- and 6-cut wool on linen. Designed and hooked by Ellen Banker, Barnard, Vermont, 2010. NEIL STEINBERG

Ellen's husband used to tell her that shoes defined people. The polka dots are repeated in the border for emphasis SCALE, CONTRAST, EMPHASIS, PATTERN, BALANCE

The Carrot Underground, 49" x 27½", #6-cut wool on linen. Designed and hooked by Ellen Banker, Barnard, Vermont, 2008. NEIL STEINBERG
The underground activity gives this rug depth and whimsy. The lines of various shades of brown emphasize the motion underground, and give the ants a baseline on which to walk. **LINE, VALUE, SCALE, MOVEMENT, EMPHASIS**

Coleus, 39" x 35½", reclaimed and new wool strips, flat hooking and proddy, on linen. Designed and hooked by Karen Kaiser, Belleville, Ontario, Canada, 2010.
The various techniques add depth and texture. Karen bases her designs and photographs on a love of plants. Instead of the usual rectangular shapes, she thought, "What if I tried to use irregular shapes to finish the design, emphasizing the subject?" **SCALE, COLOR, TEXTURE, EMPHASIS, SHAPE, CONTRAST**

44 ■ DESIGN BASICS FOR RUG HOOKERS

Island Sunrise, 14" x 68", wool strips, yarn (mohair, chenille, boucles, handspun, wool) on linen. Designed and hooked/punched by Sara Judith Nelson, British Columbia, Canada, 2010. HEATHER GOLDSWORTHY **SPACE, COLOR, VALUE, EMPHASIS**

Original inspiration for ***Coleus.*** Notice how the change in the background emphasizes the leaf.

GALLERY OF RUGS ■ 45

Philodendron, 39" x 25½", new and reclaimed wool strips, hooked and proddy, on linen. Designed and hooked by Karen Kaiser, Belleville, Ontario, Canada, 2009.

"To make the frame, my husband kindly cut the shapes I drew on plywood for me. Then he cut the centre out so it wouldn't be so heavy. I attached a 5" strip of black wool close to the edges of my hooking and hooked up to it. I stretched and stapled the backing around the wooden frame like stretching a canvas and then sewed the wool down by hand to cover the staples." SHAPE, TEXTURE, COLOR, VALUE

The March, 18" x 43", #3- and 4-cut wool on linen. Designed by Karen Kaiser and hooked by Dolores Daechsel, Scarborough, Ontario, Canada, 2009.

Dolores studied sunsets for weeks and noticed they invariably were dark at the horizon line, lightening up into the atmosphere. BALANCE, TEXTURE, MOVEMENT, VALUE, COLOR, CONTRAST, SCALE

Yorkshire Childhood, 41" x 26", wool strips, yarn (mohair, chenille, boucles, handspun, wool) on linen. Designed and hooked/punched by Sara Judith, Nelson, British Columbia, Canada, 2010.

"I enjoy combining punch hooking with traditional hooking. I find traditional hooking best for details and punch hooking excels at TEXTURE, COLOUR COMBINATIONS, AND BACKGROUNDS."

Spirit Dance, 20" x 24", alternative materials and a variety of hand cuts on burlap. Designed and hooked by Patti Armstrong, Zurich, Ontario, Canada, 2009.

Patti found immediately that she was allergic to wool fibers yet got "hooked" on this expressive medium anyway. She has been resourceful enough to test out anything that will not fall apart long enough to be hooked through at least one hole. An energetic teacher, she is known to use the washed lining material from wool garments including the interfacing material. Bright candy wrappers, nylon stockings, of course, and even reusable dish towels have found their way into some of Armstrong's workshops. **SHAPE, TEXTURE, VALUE, PATTERN, MOVEMENT**

Let the River Run, 24" x 16", wool yarn, wood, and aboriginal basket coiling on linen. Designed and hooked by Judith Stephens, Strathalbyn, South Australia, 2010.

"The title refers to the depleted Murray River which runs from Queensland down to the mouth in South Australia. Not enough rain, and too many greedy farmers along the way—irrigation where crops (rice fields and cotton) should never be sewn. The central motif (circle) is an Aboriginal symbol representing the heart, made using Aboriginal basket techniques. Inserted into the hooking are circles of wood representing the dying trees that are scattered throughout the landscape." **COLOR, TEXTURE, MOVEMENT, LINE, SHAPE**

Hillside, 29" x 20", #6-cut wool and cotton on linen. Designed and hooked by Ellen Banker, Barnard, Vermont, 2005. NEIL STEINBERG

Hillside was the Banker's home in Virginia for 17 years. It's a small historic Quaker farmhouse. Ellen picked the gold background rather than a more usual green to emphasize the flowers. This rug reminded her of a painting—no border needed.

SHAPE, SCALE, COLOR, PATTERN, MOVEMENT, SPACE

50   ■   DESIGN BASICS FOR RUG HOOKERS

TOP LEFT: *PF Colours,* 28" x 19", #4-cut wool on linen. Designed and hooked by Ingrid Hieronimus, Petersburg, Ontario, Canada, 2009.

Using her own dye recipes from *Primary Fusion*, Ingrid finds this rug is a great teaching tool for color, value and pattern. She dyed each color in a value swatch. COLOR, VALUE, PATTERN, UNITY, RHYTHM

BOTTOM LEFT: *Double Pots,* 54" x 67", #6- and 7-cut wool on linen. Designed and hooked by Christine Walker-Bird, Belleville, Ontario, Canada, 2009.

Christine designed a pot with three flowers, then reversed the design creating a different sense of balance in the central space than if it was one pot. By introducing the light background again in one of the borders, she leads our eyes outward and gives the feeling of a larger rug. SHAPE, COLOR, CONTRAST, PATTERN, BALANCE, UNITY, EMPHASIS

RIGHT: *David's Stem of Flowers,* 52" x 18", #8-, 6-, and 5-cut wool on linen. Designed for Ruckman Mill Farm and hooked by Susan L. Feller, Augusta, West Virginia, 2009.

The straight, long stem and angled branches inspired the border. By drawing a flower over the border on each side, the design encourages the viewer's eye to travel up the stem and into the outer frame. The diagonal lines are emphasized by changing values and hooking continuously to the center of each block. This technique mimics "Tramp Art" layered wood frames. LINE, VALUE, BALANCE, SPACE, BORDER

GALLERY OF RUGS ■ 51

Crop Circles, 32" x 29", #8 ½-, 8-, 6-cut and hand-torn wool on linen. Designed and hooked by Deb Lesher, Boyertown, Pennsylvania, 2009.

The design was inspired by a watercolor Deb saw in a yard sale. She carries a small sketchbook and jots sketches when something interests her. The rug was completed in a class taught by Jayne Hester, who suggested the "crop circle" effect. **SPACE, TEXTURE, LINE**

52 ■ DESIGN BASICS FOR RUG HOOKERS

Colour Theory, 50" x 28", #4-cut wool on linen. Designed and hooked by Ingrid Hieronimus, Petersburg, Ontario, Canada.

Ingrid is a master of color and pattern. She used values and the full range of the color wheel in a composition that feels as if it is rippling. Her dyeing tip is to use white nylons in place of expensive wool when experimenting with dyes.

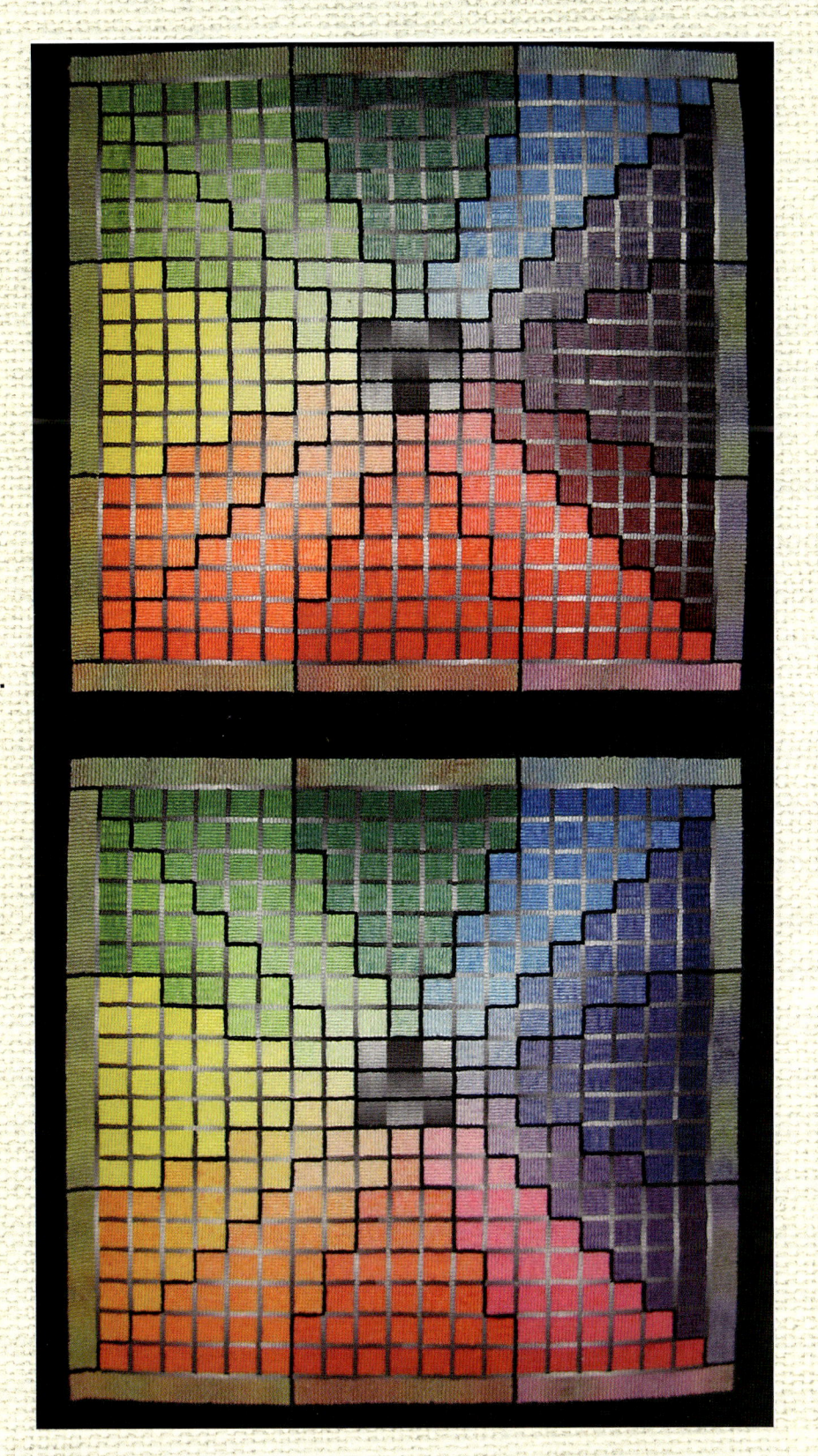

LEFT: *Big Squares, Small Squares,* 54" x 24", #8-cut wool on linen. Designed and hooked by Susan L. Feller, Augusta, West Virginia, 2006.

The design alternates a dark-feeling square with a lighter one. Each includes three different wools in the selected color, staying within the chosen value. The border is close to the size of the smallest square.

PATTERN, SHAPE, VALUE, TEXTURE, UNITY

GALLERY OF RUGS ■ 53

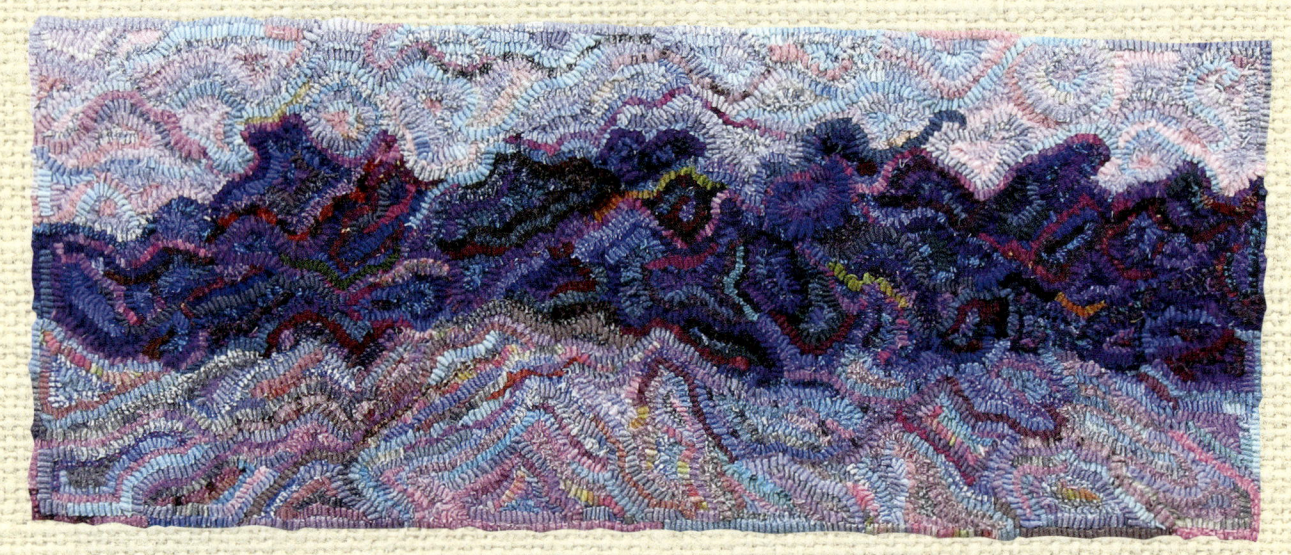

My Mountain State, 12" x 26", various cuts on linen. Designed and hooked by Susan L. Feller, Augusta, West Virginia, 2010.

This piece was an independent study you can replicate. Take your snarl bag, presorted into individual color bundles. Choose one bundle you are uncomfortable with and sort it further into light, medium, and dark values. Now select a strip and begin to hook. After the line has progressed, turn your piece in all directions and decide how to divide the space into the three different values.

Looking at this piece vertically and then horizontally, I decided there was a mountain range forming. The darkest wools were hooked into several mountains; the lightest behind, on top, as the sky, and the medium in the foreground. The direction of hooking draws the viewer back to the mountains, implying distance. On the lower right side, I sorted the medium pile further into light and dark and clustered some dark at the foot of the mountain casting a slight shadow. **COLOR, VALUE, SHAPE**

Geometric for Tamarack, 8" x 10", #6- and 8-cut wool on monk's cloth. Designed and hooked by Susan L. Feller, Augusta, West Virginia, 2010. Hooked in a warm, neutral palette of textured wools, the design has an inner section divided by diagonal lines centered on the larger plane. Random circles poke out from underneath and flow off the edge, adding to the energy. **TEXTURE, SHAPE, SPACE, MOVEMENT**

Diamonds, 33" x 48", #5- and 6-cut recycled wool on linen. Adapted from a 1970s-era colonial crafts book with antique rugs; hooked by Shirley Winklepleck, Brighton, Michigan, 2009.

A conscious decision was made to not whip the rug with a strong, solid color, because it would have stopped the energy and flow of the design. Instead Shirley carried the textured red all around the outer edge. **PATTERN, CONTRAST, RHYTHM**

Yellow Pot, 26" x 37.5", #5- and 6-cut wool on linen. Designed and hooked by Christine Walker-Bird, Belleville, Ontario, Canada, 2008.

The title color is used throughout the rug in a good balance. The concentration of yellow in the large pot anchors the design. **LINE, BALANCE, COLOR**

Rider and Friend, 27" x 24", #7-, 6-, and 5-cut wool on linen. Designed by Vermont Folk Rugs for Hooked on Ewe and hooked by Linda Harwood, Ionia, Michigan, 2009.

Linda began color planning with her favorite lime green and purple. A particular piece of textured wool inspired the addition of the golden orange. These three colors are a triad on the color wheel. By using a medium gray for the horse, the rider's garments could be strong, dark colors. **COLOR, MOVEMENT, EMPHASIS, BORDER**

56 ■ DESIGN BASICS FOR RUG HOOKERS

Papal Squares, 17" x 26", #5-cut wool on linen. Designed and hooked by Christine Walker-Bird, Belleville, Ontario, Canada, 2010.

    Overlapping squares enliven this random pattern. Light values attract the viewer to all parts and the dark edges contain the energy.
PATTERN, SHAPE, RHYTHM

Old Traditional Pattern, 32" x 52", #6- and 8-cut recycled wool on linen. Inspired by a rug in Jessie Turbayne's collection; designed (with permission) and hooked by Shirley Winklepleck, Brighton, Michigan, 2009.

    Shirley is attracted to antique rug designs and collects recycled wools to accent the old styles. She concentrates on balancing values by sorting her stash. The neutrals were spot dyed or solid ecru over camel tones. To enhance the red outline from the other parts of the circles she spot dyed those wools also.
PATTERN, CONTRAST, SHAPE, SPACE, COLOR, VALUE, TEXTURE, BALANCE

GALLERY OF RUGS

Winter in West Virginia, 26" x 18", #5- to 8-cut wool and yarns on linen with hand-dyed wool appliqué, needle felted roving, and embroidery. Designed and hooked by Susan L. Feller, Augusta, West Virginia, 2008.

Technique is one of the three legs of a good design. To achieve depth, the right side is a hand-dyed piece of wool with surface design techniques to portray the landscape. **LINE, TEXTURE, CONTRAST, SHAPE, COLOR, SPACE**

Floral Color Study, 12½" x 25", #8-cut wool on linen. Designed by Linda Pietz, Cactus Needle, California; hooked by Nola Heidbreder, St. Louis, Missouri, 2009.

Linda designed this mat to be used in workshops studying color. Nola used a different combination of colors in each square. The upper left is primary colors, then neutrals, and third complementary colors. **COLOR, SHAPE, PATTERN, VALUE**

Autumn Leaf, 25" x 20½", hand-cut, recycled cotton, wool flannel, and machine-dyed blanket on Hessian (burlap); hand-shuttled with prodded edge. Designed and hooked by Yvonne Autrie, Norfolk, England, 2009. **SCALE, CONTRAST, BORDER, SHAPE, MATERIALS**

Olympic Peninsula, 30" x 40", #4-, 5-, 6-, and 8-cuts on linen. Adapted with permission from a picture by Penny Soto and hooked by Michele Wise, Seabeck, Washington, 2009.

    This rug is a composite of nature that surrounds her home in the Pacific Northwest. Michele made nature the important part of the rug by stylizing the background using recycled grays. The rhododendron (affectionately known as rhoddy) is Washington's state flower. The Chinook salmon is their most valued fish, and the mountain goat lives in the Olympic Mountains. She put the items in their own frame in front of the areas of their natural background. The flower is an adaptation of a work by Penny Soto. The wavy lines indicate the Hood Canal and the flower is large to balance the right side of the rug. Michele used three motifs for interest and added a plain frame around the rug to enclose it. **SHAPE, SCALE, VALUE, CONTRAST, BALANCE, RHYTHM**

GALLERY OF RUGS ■ 59

60 ■ DESIGN BASICS FOR RUG HOOKERS

TOP LEFT: *Leaf Peeping Season,* 9" x 12", #5- and 6-cut wool on linen. Designed and hooked by Susan L. Feller, Augusta, West Virginia, 2010.

    This mat illustrates several lessons. Color choice was restricted to complements red and green, light and bright to dark and dull. Leading the viewer through the scene along with putting them into the picture was accomplished with the road entering at an angle and disappearing behind trees before exiting on the right. The sky is slightly spotted light cool gray and adds to the feeling of a fall day in West Virginia. **COLOR, TEXTURE, SCALE, LINE**

BOTTOM LEFT: *Rainbow of Trees,* 12" x 16", #6-cut wool and needle felting; modified triangle mounted on stretcher bars. Designed and hooked by Susan L. Feller, Augusta, West Virginia, 2010.

    In this modern interpretation of an 1846 design, the trees take on a different feeling when hooked in bright colors with a dark background. The outside shape of the hooked piece accents the stepping stone pattern. The confetti look on the right tree was achieved by needle felting the snippets from all the other trees. **COLOR, SHAPE, SCALE, PATTERN, TEXTURE**

RIGHT: *No. 2 Pencils,* 69" x 21", #6- and 8-cuts on linen. Designed and hooked by Jenny Rupp, Liberty Township, Ohio, 2010. The fringe finish distracts the viewer from the main motif—recognizing that the stripes are pencils is a humerous surprise. **PATTERNING, VALUE, SCALE, COLOR, EMPHASIS**

GALLERY OF RUGS

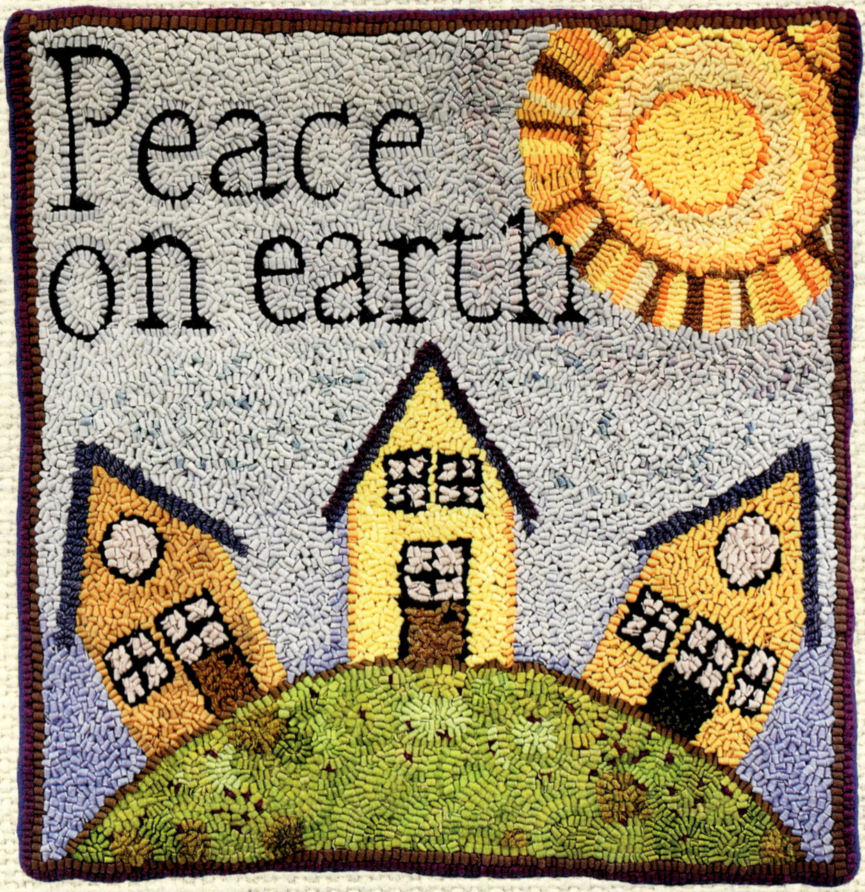
Peace
on earth

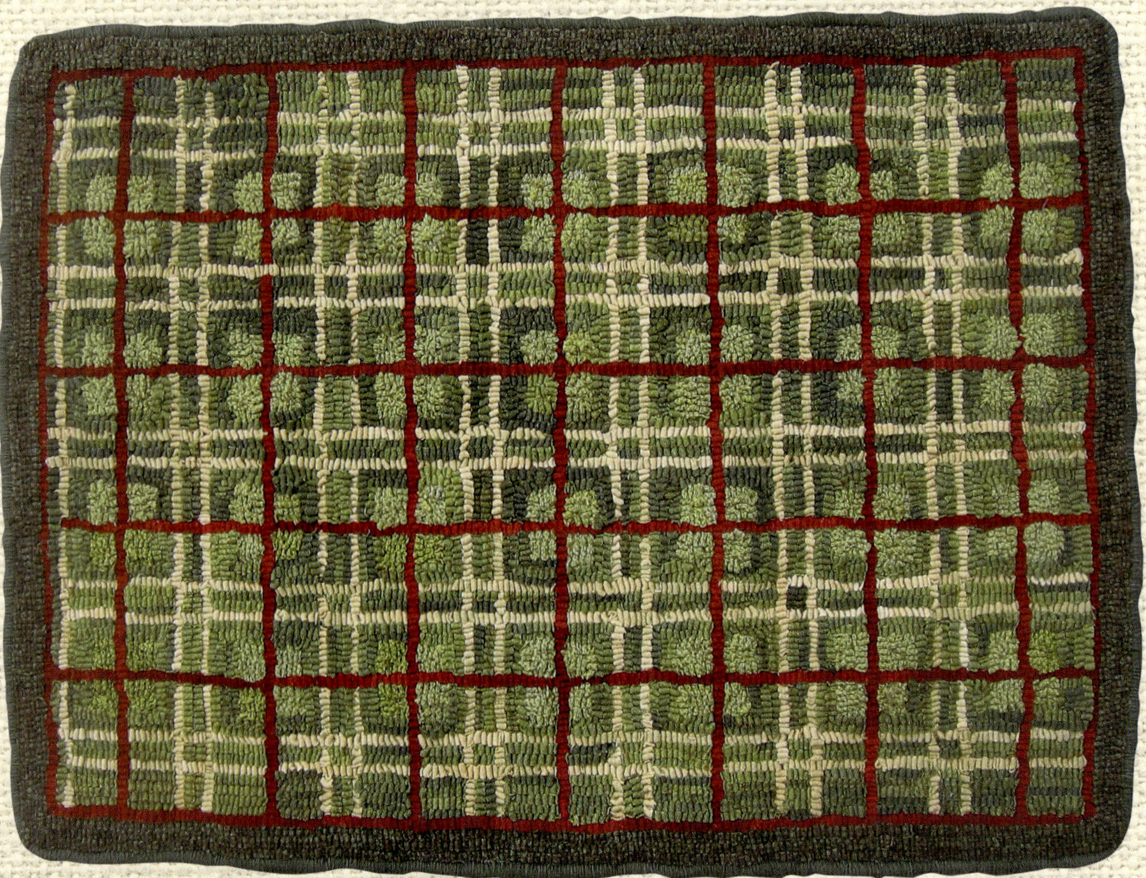

TOP LEFT: *Peace on Earth*, 24" x 24", #8-cut wool and ½" pantyhose strips on linen. Designed by Big Dog Designs and hooked by Michelle Sirois-Silver, Vancouver, British Columbia, Canada, 2010.
TEXTURE, COLOR, BALANCE, MOVEMENT

BOTTOM LEFT: *Bev's Plaid*, 21½" x 30", #8-cut wool on linen. Designed and hooked by Jerilynn Powers, Libertyville, Illinois, 2009.

Bev Conway drew one square from a larger design, *Plaid Sampler*, and Jerilynn repeated it. The complementary coloring works well in her décor.
COLOR, LINE, SHAPE, UNITY, PATTERN

RIGHT: *Lonesome Highway*, 59" x 29", #8-cut recycled and dyed wool on monk's cloth. Designed and hooked by Susan L. Feller, Augusta, West Virginia, 2003.

Drawn by Jim Lilly, this design commemorates the hundreds of miles we both traveled for years between New Jersey and West Virginia. The value changes jump along, moving the viewer, and the shapes diminish into the distance. The yellow line refers to a paved highway. **VALUE, PATTERN, LINE, MOVEMENT**

GALLERY OF RUGS ■ 63

Sweet Pea Seeds, 47" x 30", #6- and 8-cut wool on linen. Designed and hooked by Ellen Banker, Barnard, Vermont, 2010. NEIL STEINBERG

The border was created by the pea pods, spaced randomly. Originally Ellen hooked a consistent background on both sides of the pea pods, but decided that the only way to clearly define the border was to use a darker value on the outside of the rug. LINE, MOVEMENT, UNITY, BALANCE, BORDERS

Lindsey, 38" x 30", #4- and 8-cut and long lengths of wool on linen. Designed and hooked by Margaret Wenger, Lancaster, Pennsylvania, 2009.

    Margaret enjoys working in larger cuts and wanted to hook a portrait. Her 10-year-old granddaughter is portrayed larger than life. This young lady is involved regularly in the dyeing process with her grandmother. When she saw the finished piece with long locks of hair, her response was a large smile. **SCALE, FORM, CONTRAST**

GALLERY OF RUGS ■ 65

LEFT: *Maggie's Penny Runner,* 18" x 54", #6-, 7-, and 8-cut wool on linen. Designed for Ruckman Mill Farm and hooked by Susan L. Feller, Augusta, West Virginia, 2009.

This is a practical design with a central motif, the shape repeated in symmetrical balance and bordered by a repeating pattern. The colors are warm: analogous reds, oranges, and yellows with greens and warm neutral textures. **PATTERN, COLOR, TEXTURE, LINE, BALANCE, UNITY, VALUE**

TOP RIGHT: *Sensation,* 23½" x 30", #6- and 8 ½-cut wool on linen. Designed and hooked by Judy Privett, Kendallville, Indiana, 2010. MARIA AUSTIN

Hooking for just two years, Judy created a simple yet energized portrait of her favorite horse. **LINE, CONTRAST, SCALE, MOVEMENT**

BOTTOM RIGHT: *The Cutting Garden—Coneflower,* 39" x 26", #7-cut wool on linen. Adapted from a quilt design by Melinda Bula; hooked by Juliana Kapusta, Telford, New Jersey, 2009. **SCALE, SHAPE, VALUE, CONTRAST**

GALLERY OF RUGS ■ 67

Values and Textures, 16" x 12", #5- and 6-cut wool on linen; mounted on stretcher bars. Designed and hooked by Susan L. Feller, Augusta, West Virginia, 2010.

The two shapes, rectangle and tree, were found on a needlework from 1846. In this composition they have a twenty-first century feel. Changing the textured wools used in each tree created subtle changes in value from left to right. Notice the tree shape is also in *Rainbow of Trees (page 60)*.

VALUE, TEXTURE, PATTERN

CHAPTER TEN

Composition

"The minute I sat in front of a canvas, I was happy. Because it was a world, and I could do as I like in it."
—Alice Neel (1900–1984)

▶ **TIP:** Designs, no matter how simple, involve planning. You've learned about many design principles so far; select from your new arsenal of tools to create your patterns.
- Choose the main motif.
- What story are you going to tell using this motif?
- Add elements to support the story.
- Combine different elements using your design knowledge to create an exciting design.

STORYBOARD SEQUENCE

Composition is defined as an arrangement of elements using specific principles.

Using one of my designs I will take you through my creative steps.

Coming Into Town is the name of the design. My goal was to use a building from Pennsylvania German art—Frakturs—in a comical composition to convey the impression of depth and perspective.

SECTION FIVE • SKILL BUILDING

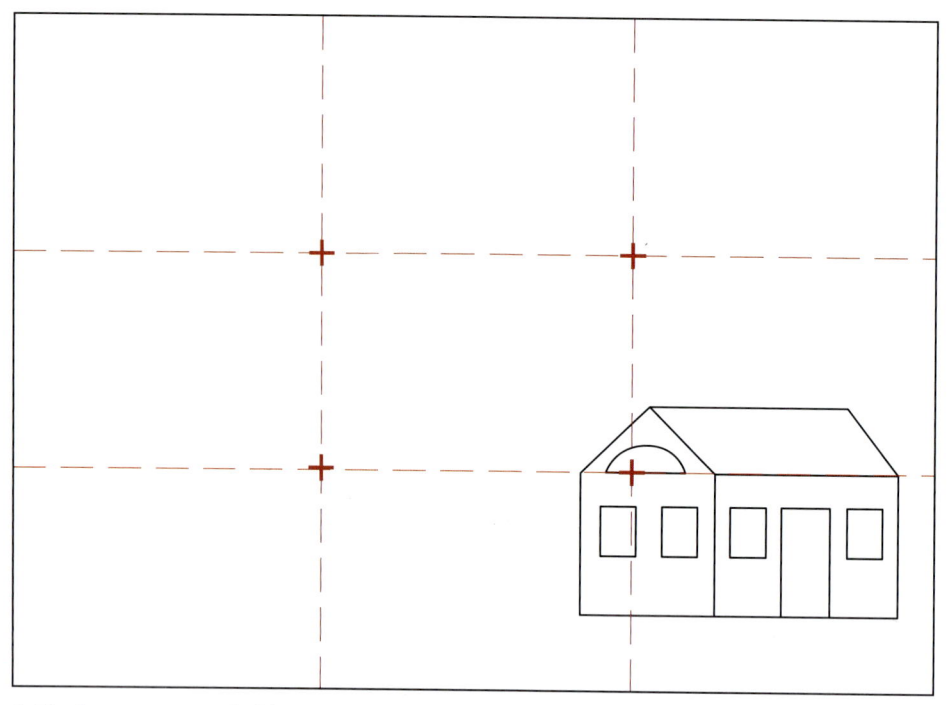

1. The first step was to decide on size and orientation. I chose 18" high x 24" wide, which included a 2" border to be developed as a frame. By dividing the remaining 14" x 20" space into thirds vertically and horizontally (making a nine-square grid), I could see the four spots of interest at the intersecting points. The building motif was the inspiration for this design. I placed it in the lower right-hand third so that the viewer's attention is drawn across the design field with plenty of space left to tell a story.

2. To offset the squared shape in the building and establish a comical element, I selected a large rounded bird and placed it to the left. I added a curved line behind the bird to establish the foreground space (note where the line meets the building—exactly at the corner). The line then comes out part of the way up the right side of the building, creating more depth. When you look at the next step, you'll see that I moved the line. What power a line has!

3. One of the goals for this pattern was to show how to achieve three dimensions in two-dimensional artwork. I placed a thinner bird standing close to the top of the hill, its skinny beak pointing to the center. I moved the curved line ½" up the left of the building to give more distance behind and more mass to the building. I added a tall slender building to the right. The steeple leads the viewer's attention to the top of the design. I drew the building so it ends at the right edge, allowing the viewer to think there is more going on beyond the "window view" of the frame border.

4. I drew road lines leading the viewer in from the border and toward a vanishing point beyond the middle. The bird stands squarely on one path; the other path comes close to the building. One more curved line portrays a distant hill. I drew the bird's tail fuller when I added the hill because it seemed to get lost among all the small shapes created by the hill and foreground lines. The question is always when to stop designing. I felt the left side still needed something as tall as the steeple. So I drew a cedar tree exactly on the top of the foreground line, extending it beyond the edge of the design. To soften the angular shapes on the right, I added a smaller tree that obscures a window and the bottom of the church. The small tree gives an impression that the church is shorter and farther away. My goal was to create movement: I did this by placing two small buildings partially viewed in the valley, and continuing the curved road winding over the top toward the distant trees.

COMPOSITION ■ 71

5. I added one more dimension: a horizontal cloud. It will be colored to show through the cutouts in the steeple. Why not add more hills . . . I drew three, one at a time, progressively larger and connecting the two sides. To emphasize depth, I added a second line to the border and mitered the corner lines.

6. Now to color plan. The building shape came directly from a Fraktur drawing in the Schwenkfelder Library, and I wanted to be true to the original in colors and the flat, folk art style. Two values of red give a very simple feeling of perspective: the front is light, the left side dark. The tall bird became red for balance. The church is textured and lighter behind the schoolhouse. Although I first hooked both trees in medium spotted wool, the right one eventually became a bold dark green because the original green was too similar to the church. I hooked the sky horizontally with two wools: one solid and the other textured, choosing wool for the clouds that was subtly lighter than the sky.

7. Here is the final rug converted in the computer to a grayscale. Study the colors and their values closely. The closer bird's tail is actually the same value as the mountain behind it, but the intensity of the orange fools our eye. The red bird is close to the sky in value. Imagine if the black line were hooked in light gray. There would not be as much definition, especially in the lower area.

CHAPTER ELEVEN

Transferring a Design

"Art does not reproduce what we see. It makes us see."
—Paul Klee (1879–1940)

Mountain Treeline, 12" x 24", #4-, 5-, and 6-cut wool and hand-dyed wool appliqué on monk's cloth. Licensed to Ruckman Mill Farm by Anne-Renée Livingston; designed and hooked by Susan L. Feller, Augusta, West Virginia, 2009.

The original piece is stained glass by Anne-Reneé Livingston, which explains the organic shapes in each tree. She leaded the glass pieces together, emphasizing the outlines. To achieve depth in the hooked version, the first plane was detailed with all the colors in small lines, followed by a quiet, light textured wool for a distant field. The nearest mountain was hooked with a dark, cool green, textured wool. This one fabric was used as two mountains. The closer one was hooked in small round shapes implying tree tops; the farther one was hooked in long horizontal lines to imply less detail in the more distant hills. The last mountain was hooked in a small textured, cool green.

The sky is a very light, hand-dyed solid piece of wool, which has some dark yellow in the upper part. It is a warmer hue than the mountains and hand-stitched tightly to the last row of hooking over the original foundation material. I appliquéd the sky to achieve more distance than a #3 (fine) cut would have suggested.

Mountain Treeline was chosen as a finalist in *Celebration XX*I. **COLOR, SHAPE, SPACE, PATTERN, RHYTHM, TEXTURE**

Learning to transfer a design to backing is an important skill. I've included one of my patterns, *Mountain Treeline*, for your own independent study. At full size, the pattern is 12" x 24". Or hook either half at 12" x 12" for a smaller version; when finished this square will cover a 14" square pillow form.

Mountain Treeline is adapted from a stained glass design by Anne-Reneé Livingston. Her stained glass piece includes a large butterfly hovering over flowers in a meadow; the tree line is the upper third of the window. The long skinny repeat has been a successful rug pattern for Ruckman Mill Farm.

Mountain Treeline, 12" x 24", #5- and 6-cut wool on linen. Hooked by Francine Even, Norwalk, Connecticut, 2010.

Francine used a subtle palette, including a spotted wool as the sky. Her approach to this design gives a feeling of a warm wet day. **COLOR, TEXTURE, VALUE**

Mountain Treeline, 12" x 24", #6-cut wool on linen. Hooked by Barbara Plunkett, Greenville, Maine, 2010.

Barbara looked at this design and personalized it. She is from Maine and lives near lakes. The trees are more appropriate to her northern region. **VALUE, SHAPE, COLOR**

Stained glass art by Anne-Renée Livingston, Virginia Beach, Virginia, 2009. My *Mountain Treeline* is inspired by the top section of this window.

Look at the three versions of *Mountain Treeline*. Notice how three different artists chose colors and fabrics and changed motifs to suit their vision, the story they wanted to tell.

What story do you want to tell in your interpretation? Change the season, hook it as if it were leaded stained glass with wools dyed to mimic stained glass, or choose different materials to change the look entirely. Add your own alterations to the pattern before you begin to transfer it to your backing.

HOW TO TRANSFER

An easy way to transfer a design to backing involves a dark permanent marker and a window on a sunny day.

1. **Prepare your pattern.** Darken all lines on your paper pattern with a fine-point marker.
2. **Draw the outer border of the pattern.** Take your backing fabric, measure at least 3" from the edge, and place the point of the marker in the groove formed between two threads. Drag the marker toward yourself, staying in the groove. If the marker jumps out of that groove, you will feel it happen. Get back in the groove before you continue. Draw all of the straight lines of your pattern onto the backing, confirming the measurements with your paper pattern.
3. **Trace the pattern.** Now tape the paper pattern to the window. Position the backing fabric over the pattern, lining up the predrawn borders. Tape the backing to the window. This alignment will guarantee that your weave is straight and that the pattern will be on the straight of the grain. Trace all the other parts of your pattern using the marker.

TRANSFERRING A DESIGN

CHAPTER TWELVE

Borders, Finishing, Framing Tips

"Creativity takes courage." —Henri Matisse (1869–1954)

Sweet Pea Seeds, detail. (See the full rug on page 64.)

Double Pots, detail. (See the full rug on page 50.)

Big Squares, Small Squares, detail. (See the full rug on page 52.)

BORDERS AS DESIGN ELEMENTS

Many rug designs include a frame or **border**. A border serves the same purpose as a picture frame. Thin curving lines can establish a gentle border; a straight line mimics a frame.

Sometimes a border is practical. Perhaps you want to extend the size of the rug: you could use smaller replicas of motifs repetitively to move the viewer's eye around. Selecting colors from the body adds interest.

As sources for ideas, look at dinnerware, patterned tablecloths, bed linens, and picture frames. Depending on the style of your rug, you may have several borders that vary in widths but together build a

Square: *Finish Variation*

supporting edge around the central design. Examine picture frames closely and notice how some are composed of a series of different widths with varying decorative details, alternating geometric and organic shapes. If you find one that appeals to you and you think it might translate well to a rug border, sketch it in your journal.

Many great artists use the border as another field, an additional area for design. Degas would paint a dancer going off the edge of his canvas. Framed, the work seems to be viewed through a window. His border makes us consider more than the figure. When our rugs are on the floor, borders emphasize space, extending into the room space rather than restricting it.

FINISHING AS DESIGN

Your choice of **finishing** technique is also a design element. When I am working with a student on a design, I ask how they want to finish the rug. If an edge is whipped, the color of that small bit of yarn at the edge of the rug is part of the design. If you plan to turn the backing and sew binding tape to the back, you may want to hook a dark line or two as a final contrasting frame. Sewing on a show binding could add an inch or so of a beautiful plaid or textured wool. Some rug hookers who choose this binding hook a thin contrasting last row to emphasize the edge.

Autumn Leaf, detail. (See the full rug on page 59.)

▶ **TIP:** Borders may incorporate a saying or message. The choice of font is very important to the overall effect. Cursive fonts are active and feminine. Vertical and block fonts can feel static, or boldly call attention and be interpreted as masculine.

SELECTING A FRAME

If you have not framed artwork before, study framed art before you go to the framer. Look at framed pieces wherever you go—in restaurants, stores, on TV, and in magazines. Visit local art shows where the artists have framed pieces. You may even see instances when a frame distracts from the art.

Textiles are different from paper and canvas. The texture, weight, and luster of the fibers are important considerations. For example, fabric-wrapped mats complement hooked art better than paper matting. If you choose to glaze the hooked piece, use UV-filtered material and be sure the glazing is separated from the fibers to eliminate moisture building up.

Properly framing a hooked piece is tricky. There are a lot of decisions to be made along the way. When in doubt, use a professional experienced in framing textiles.

Remember that a line is a basic element and can be used here to complete the design. Your choice of width, color, value, or type of wool will change the overall complexion of a rug. Consider the final shape of your piece. Yvonne Autrie and Karen Kaiser each made the shape of their leaf the final border (pages 59 and 46). In *Rainbow of Trees* (page 60), the progressive increase in size is emphasized by an angled edge, and the piece is mounted on a rectangle of the same value. And you can enhance a design by repeating a shape in a smaller scale or different color, thus using several principles (pattern, scale, color) in a final border.

HANGING YOUR HOOKED PIECE

There are several ways to hang art on the wall, depending on the rug's size and overall weight: add a sleeve, attach it to carpet tack strips, mount it on fabric and stretch it around a board or support, or lace it and place it inside a picture frame.

Sleeves

A common technique is to hand stitch a cotton **sleeve** on the back along the top that ends about an inch from each end. This sleeve hides the wooden dowel, metal conduit rod, or flat length of wood used as the hanger.

Framing tools. Common hardware tools can be used to present your craft as art.
- Screw eyes
- Braided wire
- Picture hanging hooks
- Artist stretcher bars
- Staple gun
- Frameboard

> **TIP:** If you are hanging your rugs, be sure to rotate them at least quarterly, taking one rug down and hanging another. This planned switch will give the stressed fibers rest and remove the rug from light exposure. When you hang rugs, they will eventually begin to roll along the sides because fabric is hygroscopic, meaning it absorbs humidity. The backing fabric also reacts to the stress of our loops. If your rug begins to roll, take the rug down and steam it flat again. Another way to keep the rug flatter is to add a sleeve and rod at the bottom.

Nails or brackets can be attached to the wall to hang the rod. Another option is to put screw eyes in the end of the wooden rod, attach wire or fishing line to these screw eyes, and hang it from a hook higher up the wall.

To make the sleeve, measure the circumference of the rod and add a little extra. Use muslin or cotton, not wool, because wool will stretch. Turn under ½" at both the top and bottom of the fabric for neat finished edges. Place the sleeve about 1" from the top of the rug. Pin the sleeve in place, and hand stitch along the top edge: be sure to catch the foundation material, not just the hooked loops. Insert the rod, wrapping the sleeve fabric snugly around it. Leave a little slack, pin, and hold your work up by the rod to see how it hangs. Make sure the sleeve doesn't show above the rug and that any bend in the rod is minimal. You don't want the rug to be pulled around the rod and distorted. If you are satisfied, stitch the bottom edge of the sleeve to the back of the rug, being careful to catch the backing in the stitches.

Your choice of support is very important. Wooden dowels are available at hardware stores in a variety of widths. The smaller ones will flex if you use them to hang heavy pieces. You could cut a slit halfway across the sleeve to accommodate a third nail and eliminate flexing of a smaller rod, or use a flat 2"-wide strip of wood instead of a round rod. You might use a metal rod (conduit), which you can find in the electrical department, usually with screwed ends. PVC pipe is another option.

Carpet Tack Strips

An easy display system to hang rugs, especially if you rotate your rugs, is to mount **carpet tack strips** to your wall. This method works well if your rugs are a common size. You can purchase single strips at a hardware store. Make sure you mount the board with the teeth angled up so they grip your rug's backing. Repeatedly removing and hanging the rug may damage the backing, so be careful to settle it onto the teeth gently, imbedding the teeth firmly into the backing, not just into the loops.

Stretching

Antique collectors often display frail rugs by mounting them on a dark fabric-covered board or artist canvas. This method doesn't put undue stress on the actual rug.

Here's how to proceed. Let's use a common 24" x 36" rug as our example. For the backing, either purchase a pre-wrapped artist canvas (28" x 40"), or two sets of 28" and 40" artist stretcher bars and a piece of $^3/_{16}$"-thick acid-free foam core, cut to size. When mounted, 2" of the backing fabric will show all around the rug; you can make it wider or narrower depending upon your preferences and the rug's location. Select a solid-colored poplin or duck cloth (heavy-weight cotton), choosing either black or a very dark neutral. Remember that black enhances colors. Cut the piece of cloth another 4" or 5" larger all around, as you will stretch it around the frame and staple it to the back.

First, iron the backing fabric to eliminate any folds or wrinkles. Put the stretcher bars together and staple or glue the foam core to them, making sure the edges are flush and your staples are long enough to enter the wood. The staples should be flush with the board; any protrusions will show as bumps under the fabric.

Finish your rug as you normally would, with whipped or bound edges. Then lay your rug, face up, in the center of the fabric and put the assembled frame underneath to confirm that you have enough fabric to stretch around back. Remove the frame and meticulously hand stitch all around the piece—through the rug and backing fabric—between the whipping (edge) and the hooking. I find it easiest to sit at a table and use a tabletop to support the rug. In this position, I am able to look at both the underside and top of the rug while I stitch.

Now put the mounted rug back on the support frame, center the backing fabric, and flip the entire package over. Begin to "stretch" the fabric by selecting one side at the middle and stapling it to the back of the bar. Pull tightly on the opposite side and staple it in

> **TIP:** Remember that stretcher bars are available in whole inch lengths. A custom support frame could be built by a carpenter if needed. Show them a stretcher bar for suggestions on construction.

▶ **TIP:** *The Artist's Way*, a well-regarded book on design and thinking artistically, suggests that you take yourself and a friend on an art date. Nearly any destination will work; it doesn't have to be called an "art space." Take along a journal, a pencil, and an inquisitive attitude. When the day is over, exchange interpretations and insights from your trip and learn from each other.

place. Do the same with the other two sides. Turn the contraption over and review your work; if you need to adjust a staple, take it out and pull more, or pull less. Make sure to get the positioning and tension just right before you move on to the next step.

Go to each corner and fold the fabric in at an angle. Staple, then carefully miter and staple each corner, creating as little bulk as possible. Take one long side and divide one section in half; staple, then repeat on the opposite side. Repeat this process all around the frame; the back-and-forth will guarantee even stretch-

▶ **TIP:** The depth of the frame you choose must be deep enough to accommodate the rug, backer, closing, glazing (if you select to add it), and a spacer to keep the fibers away from the glass by at least ¼".

ing. Find a friend to help you—this task is ideal for two people and two staple guns.

Because the hooking adds a lot of weight to the mounting, the stitching around the edges will not be enough to hold your rug flat. It will need to be reinforced. Take a crochet-weight thread and stitch between loops, through the backing and mounting fabric, and through the foam core or canvas backing in a series of random, widely spaced stitches. The stitches don't have to be very close, but you do need to keep the thread taut. A zigzag pattern is best. Tie off your thread securely.

To add the hanging equipment, choose two screw eyes and measure one third of the way down from the top on each side. Install the eyes there. Cut a length of picture wire long enough to arch up to just about the top of the frame between the screw eyes. Loop one end of the wire into the eye, pull it around and through

80 ■ DESIGN BASICS FOR RUG HOOKERS

An early morning in November in Clayton, Indiana. This dramatic composition has subtle coloring, an off-centered focal point reaching out of the frame, a dark foreground, and lines of light stubble directing your eye to the forested horizon.

again, then twist the excess about three inches up the long part of the wire. If you are using an actual picture hanger, test where the wire will fall when hanging, tighten the other side, and cut off the excess wire.

Label the foam core with the title of your rug and other important information. (You also put a label on the back of the rug, right?) This hanging method is the least invasive for your rug, and years from now preservationists will appreciate the care you took.

Lacing

If your piece is small (less than 24" square), you could use a technique common to needlework called **lacing**. In lacing, you use a continuous thread, repeatedly pulling the needle through opposite sides of the backing fabric from one side to the other to encase the stretcher bars and foam core underneath.

Before beginning to lace, you need to figure out the final size of your mounted piece. When you are done hooking and before you do any type of finishing, pull on your foundation fabric, making it taut so you can measure the exact width and length of the hooked area. This method assumes you are going to add a picture frame, so allow room for the rabbet (lip of the frame) to overlap or hide about ¼" of your hooking. If you don't want to lose any loops, you have two choices: hook an extra ¼" at the edge of your piece, or make the size of the stretcher bars ¼" wider so the backing will be under the frame. Note: This second method means the edge of the frame will sit lower than your loops.

Select and construct the stretcher bars, then staple acid-free foam core, cut to size, to the face. Lay your work face down on a flat surface, then position the support frame evenly over the piece with the acid-free board

1. Lacing supplies.

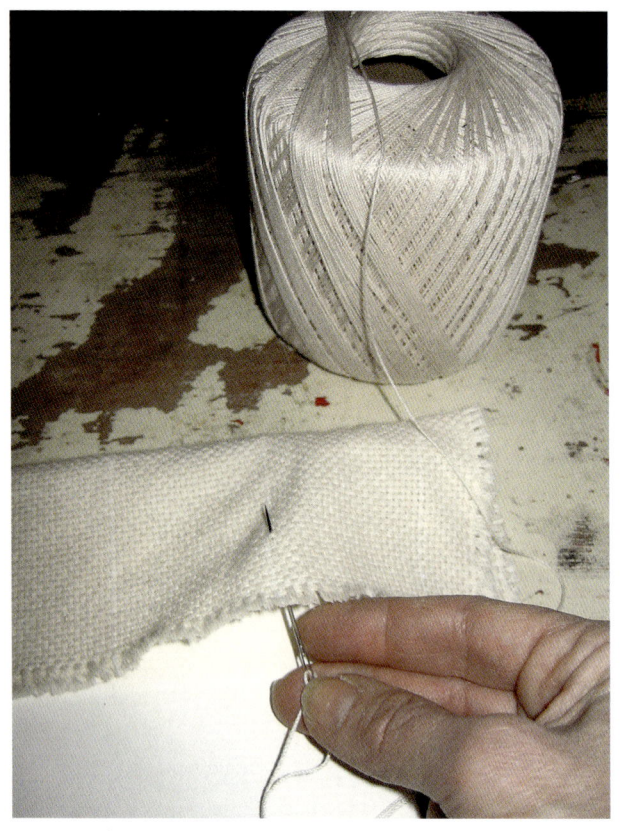

2. Lacing begins on one corner of the backing.

3. The thread is pulled across the back of the frame.

4. Fold the corners and continue to the bottom of the frame. Repeat the process on the other two sides.

82 ■ DESIGN BASICS FOR RUG HOOKERS

The edge of the mat disappears under the rabbet. Keep this in mind as you decide on your design, and later as you choose a frame. Usually 1/4" is hidden under the edge of the frame.

In a floating mount, the edge of the mat is exposed.

touching your work. Check the positioning from the front before starting to lace.

Determine the weight of the thread by choosing one that will break before your backing fabric rips but is strong enough to be pulled and keep tension. Crochet cotton is usually a good choice. With a threaded needle begin at one corner, about 1/2" in from the edge. Enter the backing fabric and draw excess thread off the spool as the needle continues to the lower side. Enter the backing fabric on the lower side and return again to the opposite edge, about 1/4" away from your starting point.

Continue in this zigzag fashion across the piece, using a continuous length of thread. You will have to pull more thread off the spool and move the slack along to make your long stitches. When at the opposite end, knot the thread, then check the position of your work on the support before gradually tightening the string back to the starting point. Cut the spool free and tie this end of the thread loosely. Look at the front: reposition any section to make the rug square, and go back to retightening, making sure each length of thread is taut before taking up more slack on the next. This step should sound like you are plucking a stringed instrument. Now tie off the thread tightly. Fold the corners over smoothly; there will be some bulk here, so you'll need to choose a frame with enough depth to hide the extra bulk. Repeat the lacing on the other two sides.

You are now ready to add the picture frame. Do not scrimp because of cost. The frame also hides the mechanics involved in presenting your artwork.

SELECTING A PICTURE FRAME

In selecting a frame your experiences with borders will come in handy. Remember, the frame has several purposes:

- To present the work on the wall
- To enhance the design of the artwork
- To emphasize a design style
- To provide contrast

There are thousands of picture frames to choose from, but like all the other choices you have made, only three or four will be best. A framer will ask you some questions: Where will it hang? What features do you want to enhance? You don't want the framer to experiment on your hours of labor. Ask to see some other fiber art they have framed, like needlework. Rug hooking is not an everyday item and should be intriguing to a professional framer. If you don't feel comfortable with his answers, go elsewhere. Picture framing is expensive, but don't sacrifice any of these steps and settle for a cheaper frame.

Consider framing one of your pictorials or antique finds—and enjoy the results. Rug hooking isn't just for the floor!

IN CONCLUSION

My goal was to teach you a basic vocabulary about design. If you have learned by reading, seeing, and working, I know you will be looking around with new eyes. Now when a FED EX truck passes me, I see the arrow in the negative space formed between the E and X: the shape jumps out at me. The TARGET logo is memorable—no words needed. I color plan along with nature, searching for color complements and finding a perfect blue sky and orange sassafras tree line. Walking through the aisles at Lowe's, I notice that the directional signs are white background with bold blue letters, and the aisle signage is reversed. (I find the large white ones are more readable.) I am seeing and recognizing the basic elements and principles of design.

   Design is everywhere you go. Open your eyes and enjoy the show. Look for the trees in the forest wherever you are, and then show them to the world in your art. Enjoy the process and the opportunities.

Illustrated Glossary

GLOSSARY

COLOR
SHAPE
SPACE
HUE
PATTERN
RHYTHM
TEXTURE
UNITY
FORM
BALANCE
VALUE
LINE
MOVEMENT

85

art: a skill acquired by experience, study, or observation; the conscious use of skill and creative imagination especially in the production of aesthetic objects.

artist: one who professes and practices an imaginative art; one skilled or versed in learned arts, artisan.

balance: The eye perceives weights being equal and balanced when they have the same value or intensity of color creating harmony.

A **border** serves the same purpose as a picture frame. Often the need is decorative.

color is a combination of light rays reflected from a surface. In order to see color, there must be a light source. Notice that color is less discernable when a light is dimmed and then turned off. Color has three characteristics: hue, value, and intensity.

contrast is a design principle that provides visual interest.

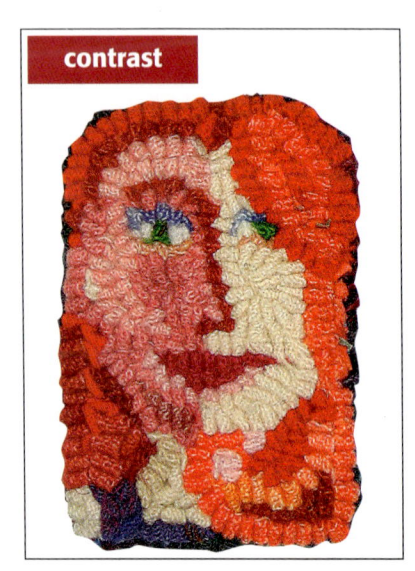

craft: a skill in planning, making, or executing, dexterity. Or an occupation or trade requiring manual dexterity or artistic skill (crafts such as pottery and sewing).

craftsman (or woman): a workman who practices a trade or handicraft, artisan; one who creates or performs with skill or dexterity especially in the manual arts.

elements: the building blocks of design. Line, shape, form, space, value, texture, and color.

emphasis refers to areas of interest that guide the eye into and out of the image through the use of a sequence of focal points.

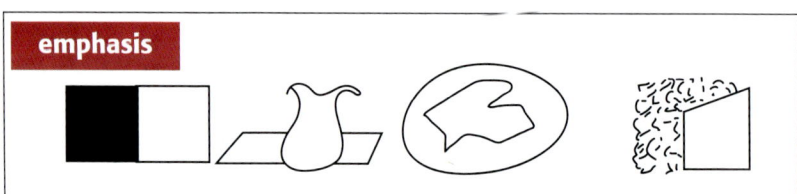

86 ■ DESIGN BASICS FOR RUG HOOKERS

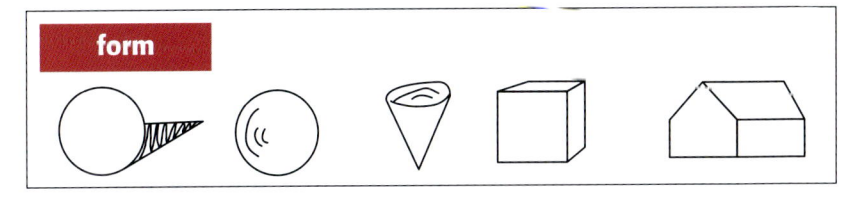

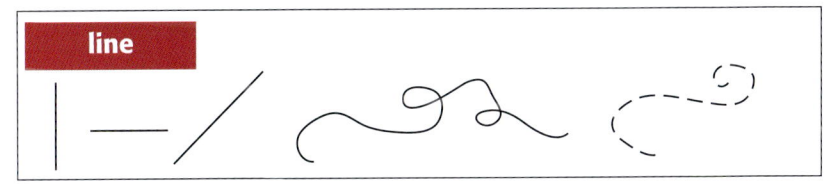

form: is any three-dimensional object. Form can be measured from top to bottom (height), side to side (width), and from back to front (depth). Form is also defined by light and dark.

hue: the wavelength, the name given to a color… red, orange, yellow, green, blue, indigo, violet.

intensity or saturation determines the brightness or dullness of a color.

lacing: a picture-framing technique used to stretch needlework for presentation.

line: a joining of points along a surface.

monochromatic: using only one color family.

movement: can be achieved with a consistent directional line or a series of lines.

negative space: space created around a motif and the edge of a design.

neutral: void of color. Fabric ranging from light to dark, either in "cool" black or "warm" browns.

pattern: in art, a pattern is defined as a single unit of design used in repetition.

positive space: the area in a design covered by a motif.

primary colors: red, blue, and yellow, the colors from which all other colors can be created using different proportions.

principles: combining the elements of design for specific effects: contrast, balance, unity, rhythm, movement, pattern, and emphasis.

rhythm: a principle used to organize a composition and create interest, unity or emphasis. Visual rhythm is achieved in the same way—repeating a shape, color or line in a regular pattern.

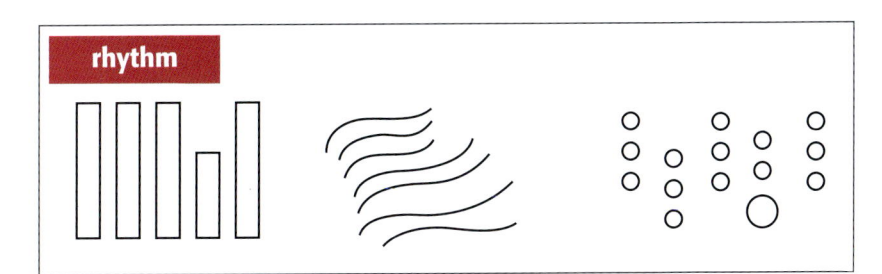

GLOSSARY AND RESOURCES ■ 87

shapes: created by joining lines. They are two dimensional.

space: the area provided for a particular purpose. It may have two dimensions (length and width), such as a floor, or it may have three dimensions (length, width, and height). Space includes the background, foreground, and middle ground.

texture: the quality of a surface. In visual art, there are two types of texture: tactile and implied.

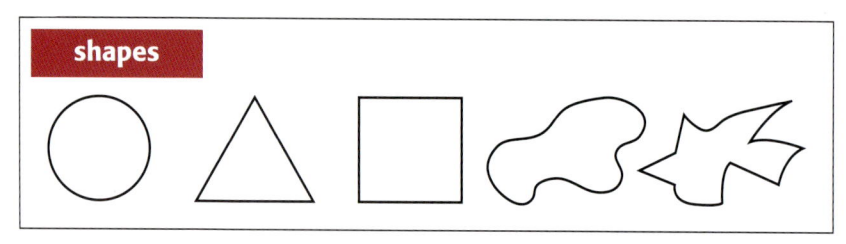

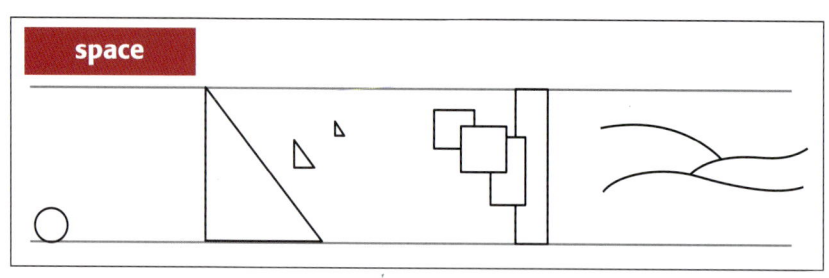

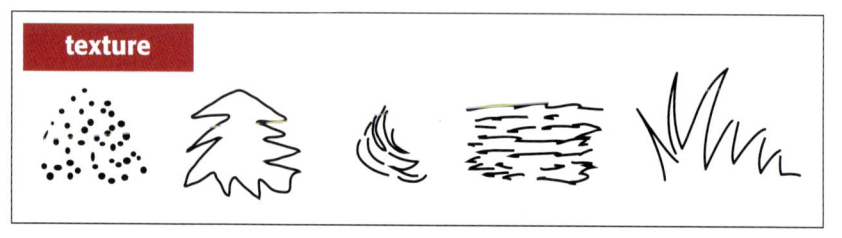

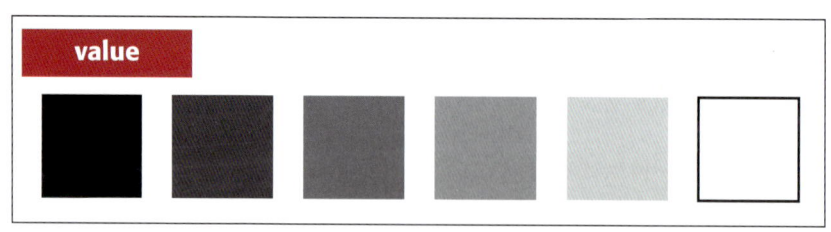

unity: a sense that everything in a piece of work belongs there, and makes the piece whole. It is achieved by the use of balance, repetition, and/or design harmony.

value: an element of art referring to the relationship between light and dark on a surface or object. Value helps create form.

88 ■ DESIGN BASICS FOR RUG HOOKERS

Resources

FURTHER READING

RHM books by Deanne Fitzpatrick, Betty Krull, Anne-Marie Littenberg, Gene Shepherd, Jane Halliwell Green, Gail Dufresne, and Cynthia Norwood. *www.rughookingmagazine.com*

A Knitter's Guide to Color, Laura Bryant, DVD, *www.interweavestore.com*

A Passion for the Creative Life: Textiles to Lift the Spirit, Mary Sheppard Burton, Sign of the Hook Books, *www.marysburton.com*

Art and Visual Perception (50th anniversary edition), Rudolf Arnheim, University of California Press, 2004.

Art + Quilt, Lyric Kinard, Interweave Press, 2009, *www.interweavestore.com*

Artforms, Duane and Sarah Preble (4th edition), HarperCollins Publishers, 1989.

Artist to Artist, compiled by Clint Brown, Jackson Creek Press, 1998.

Basic Picture Framing, Stackpole Books, 2005.

Color, Victoria Finlay, Ballantine Books, 2002.

Color and Fiber, Patricia Lambert, Barbara Staepelaere, Mary G. Fry, Schiffer Publishing, 1986.

ColorWorks, Deb Menz, Interweave Press, 2004.

Exploring Visual Design, Joseph A. Gatto, Albert W. Porter, Jack Selleck, Davis Publications, 2000.

Islamic Patterns, Keith Critchlow, Thames and Hudson, London, England, 1976 and 2004.

Masters Art Quilts, Martha Sielman, Lark Books, Sterling Publishing, 2008.

Pattern, William Justema, New York Graphic Society, 1976.

The Art Spirit, Robert Henri, Lippinott, 1923.

The Artist's Way, Julia Cameron, Jeremy P. Tarcher/Putnam, 1992.

The Group of Seven and Tom Thomson, David P. Silcox, Firefly Books, 2003.

You Can Do It!, Lauren Catuzzi Grandcolas, Herter Studio, and Chronicle Books, 2005.

DESIGNERS

Artworks by Karen Kaiser
526 Moira St. W, Belleville, ON K8N 4Z2
www.artworksbykarenkaiser.net
613-966-2658
hooking.kaiser@gmail.com

Nancy Jewett, Fluff and Peachy Bean Designs
595 Maple Street, Salisbury, VT 05769
www.fluffpeachybeandesigns.com
802-352-4722
ndjewett@myfairpoint.net

Stephanie Allen-Krauss, Green Mountain Hooked Rugs
2838 County Road, Montpelier, VT 05602
www.GreenMountainHookedRugs.com
802-223-1333
vtpansy@greenmountainhookedrugs.com

Linda Harwood, Hooked on Ewe/Vermont Folk Rugs
5339 S State Road, Ionia, MI 48846
616-527-1079
www.harwoodhookedonewe.com

The House of Price, Primco
177 Brickyard Road, Mars, PA 16046-3001
1-877-784-4665
rughook@earthlink.net

Susan L. Feller, Ruckman Mill Farm
PO Box 409, Augusta, WV 26704
www.RuckmanMillFarm.com or *www.ArtWools.com*
304-496-8073
rugs2wv@yahoo.com

Michelle Sirois-Silver, Big Dog Rugs,
1937 East 3rd Avenue,
Vancouver, British Columbia V5N 1H4
www.michellesirois-silver.com
www.bigdogrugs.com
604-253-4372
bigdogrugs@yahoo.ca

PROFESSIONAL ORGANIZATIONS/MEDIA/ EDUCATIONAL STUDIES/EXHIBITS

ATHA, Association of Traditional Hooking Artists *www.atharugs.com*

www.Colourlovers.com palettes, patterns, colour planning. Online group: fiber arts and artists

National Guild of Pearl K. McGown Rughookrafters, Inc. *www.mcgownguild.com*

OHCG, Ontario Hooking Craft Guild *www.ohcg.org*

Rug Hooking Magazine *www.rughookingmagazine.com*

Handweavers Guild *www.weavespindye.org*

Augusta Heritage Center, Elkins, West Virginia *www.augustaheritage.com*; traditional Appalachian crafts and music, weeklong classes

John C. Campbell Folk Art School, North Carolina *www.folkschool.org*; traditional crafts including rug hooking

Loyalist College, Belleville, Ontario, Canada Summer Program *www.loyalistfocus.com*; Fibre arts weeklong sessions, Continuing Education

Sauder Village—Rug Hooking Week *www.saudervillage.org*; exhibit, workshops, classes, vendors

Schwenkfelder Library and Museum, Pennsburg, PA *www.schwenkfelder.org*; resource for designs inspired by folk art in archives

St. Lawrence College, Ontario, Canada *www.stlawrencecollege.ca*; certificate in Fibre Arts concentration in rug hooking

Surface Design Journal *www.surfacedesign.org*

Textile Museum, Toronto, Ontario, Canada *www.textilemuseum.ca*

TIGHR, The International Guild of Handhooking Rugmakers *www.tighr.net*

SUPPLIES

The Color Wheel *www.colorwheelco.com*

Dorr Mill Store *www.dorrmillstore.com*; supplies, wools, patterns, workshops

Green Mountain Hooked Rugs *www.GreenMountainHookedRugs.com*; hand-dyed wools along with hundreds of bolts of new wools, patterns, supplies, restoration service, school, retreat, workshops

Majic Carpet Dyes *www.LetsHookRugs.com*; wash-fast acid dyes manufactured in Canada, available internationally

Primary Fusion *www.rughookinghome.com*; dye recipes, instructions. Ragg Tyme Studio, 66 Woodbridge Dr. RR2, Petersburg, ON N0B 2H0, 519-578-0826 *raggtyme@rughookinghome.com*

Pro-Chem *www.ProChemical.com*; wash-fast acid dyes, dyeing supplies, books

Raggety Jays Designs *http://ausrugcrafters.com*; Australian suppliers of rughooking tools. Judith Stephens designs and Jo Franco, teacher

The Wool Studio *www.thewoolstudio.com*; textured and solid wools milled especially for the rug hooker